1

For my grandchildren
Hayley, Zoey, Oliver, Charlotte, Zelda, Keegan, Ari,
and Ashlynn
Always remember, Grandma loves you bunches!
JDR

To Katelyn, Brody, and Teddy, I'm looking forward
to our years together! Papa
SAJ

A special thanks to our focus group for all of your
input, comments, and suggestions

Diane,

To my friend FROM the PAST!
Thank you for your support
God Bless

[signature]

Diane,

Thank you for your
support! Rejoice in the
daily blessings.

Jacquie

11/23/19

Table of Contents

A special thanks to Paula Aurino who helped select Bible verses which spoke to her during her readings.

Bible verses were selected from NIV New International Bible, Kings James Bible, and The New American Catholic Bible.

Prayers of Gratitude

I have been extremely blessed to have so many caring and loving people in my world. I give thanks and praise above all our Lord God who has given me a miracle and allowed me the opportunity to spread his message of unconditional love.

I also want to thank my loving wife, Terri Johnson. Without her I do not think I would have been able to succeed in this journey. She truly stood by me in sickness and in health.

To my family, Bryan and Sharlet Johnson, Brad Johnson, Butch and Nancy Johnson, Stacy Lucas, Aaron Johnson, Brad Tippett, Sherry and Dave Smith, Walter Smith, Pam and Jeff Threet, Steven Threet thank you all for being there for me and being an example of how families come together in times of need. I love you all.

Dr. Issam and Cathy Nemeh, thank you for showing me the way back to allow me the honor to receive this miracle.

Dana and Judge Duncan Beagle without your love and friendship I hate to think where my family and I would be right now. Our friendship has literally saved my life.

I'd also like to extend a special prayer of appreciation and thanks to John Montney, Pat Doyle, Mike Dunn, Pastor Jim Reid, Pat and Julie McKenna, Dave Belanger, Danny Martin, Cathy Hintz, Denny Simnitch, Cathy and Roger Epperson, Lena and Randy Epperson, Diane Epperson, Tina

McKenzie, Amy Sears, Beth Montney, Joe Ragnone, Mark and Debbie Zokoe, Sandy Sellers, Mike Swartz, John Shelton, James Horton, Roger and Charlotte Foutch, Jim Fuller, Tim Mowry, Dr. Paul Adams, Ryan Slocum, Angie Hendershot, Brendan Savage, Karen and Keith Sperling, George Hamo, Cal Ter Har, Tom Rau, Keith Richardson, Frank Mar, Bryan Illig, Curt Lowe, James (Woody) Bucherie, Mark Uyl, the Carman Talk Prayer Warriors, my 2500 Facebook Prayer Warriors, Genesys/Hurley Cancer Institute, the nurses at Genesys Hospital, the Genesee County Coaches and Officials Association and all of the people who attended my cancer fund-raiser.

For agreeing to take on this project so that my wife and I can share my story to all, I want to give a special thanks to the author, Jacquie Duff-Richardson.

There are so many people I would like to thank personally, so many people who prayed for me and my family. People I didn't even know, my wife and I thank you from the bottom of our hearts. Please know that you are in our every prayer.

Jesus Christ is the same yesterday and today, yes and forever
Hebrews 13:8

Introduction

Cancer affects every American in one way or another. Whether it is in the form of a loved one's diagnosis, a neighbor, co-worker, or oneself, cancer has a far-reaching impact. Sadly, there is no safe zone. It has been said that this disease isn't prejudiced; it doesn't discriminate against race, religion, gender or socioeconomic identity.

The array of emotions a person with cancer and their family goes through is like being on a rollercoaster ride through Hell. The fear of death and leaving loved ones behind is never ending. And then there is anger. Anger which is often directed at God. "How could God let this happen?" is often asked, especially when cancer victimizes a child. The questions far outnumber the answers.

As Christians we are taught that God has a purpose and plan for everything and that it is not our place to question Him, but to trust in Him. Some have chosen to shun the church to punish God for their illness, as if our rejection would force God into reversing this illness. Having faith is often the hardest thing to do when faced with a life-threatening disease, especially if you are told there is no cure.

The news and entertainment industry bombard people with stories on causes of cancers, cures for cancer, even celebrities fighting cancer. Cancer treatments and prevention centers have commercials during prime time viewing promoting new drugs and possibilities.

In the early 1970's, the Red Dye scare had people worrying about cancer-causing foods. Russian scientists discovered that FD&C Red Dye #2 caused malignant tumors in female mice. This dye was commonly used in many everyday food products. The public outcry to ban any and all products containing this dye caused Mars Incorporated to stop making red M & M candies, even though they never used FD&C Red Dye #2. These red candies would not reappear for another 10 years.

Other products have been linked, whether factually or not, as causing cancer. Cigarettes are possibly the most thought of cancer-causing products. It amazes people when someone who smokes like the proverbial chimney escapes cancer's clutches, while someone who has never smoked a day in their lives gets lung cancer, like Steve Johnson.

*And be not conformed to this world: but be ye
transformed by the renewing of your mind*
Romans 12:2

Chapter One

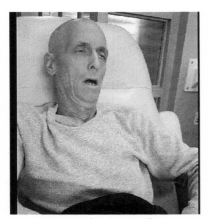

Steve Johnson 114lbs.

Six months prior to this picture, Steve was a happy, healthy 62-year-old man in a body that defied age. He was a husband, father, and grandfather. "I'm just a regular guy, who had a bad thing happen to me," he later would say of his battle with cancer.

Had you asked Steve before the summer of 2016 if he believed in miracles, Steve probably would have given you his crooked smile and said, "Hell yeah I believe in miracles!

I watched the 1980 Winter Olympics," and then laughed at his own joke. That has always been Steve's style; he brings humor and laughter to all who encounter him. He has a joke or funny story for every situation and the ability to make others laugh along with him. Heartbroken over the death of his mother, he stood to give the eulogy. Staring at him was a sea of grief-stricken faces of his family and longtime family friends. People who had grown up in the neighborhood knowing the kindness of Billie Marie Johnson. Steve stood before these people, cleared his throat and solemnly began, "My mother never had a bad word to say about anyone...except for me and my buddy, Woody Bucherie." Laughter and knowing head nods replaced the sadness for a moment. It is next to impossible to not be affected by his personality. Little did he know that his humor and positive attitude would be crucial to his experiencing the miracle which would save his life an inspire countless other people.

If you ask Steve today if he believe in miracles, he will tell you that he has personally been on a journey with God and knows that miracles are there for those who want to open their hearts to accept them.

Steve is well-known throughout the high school referee community in Genesee and surrounding counties. For 42 years Steve spent most of his time on the sports scene. He is one of the most respected officials in the state of Michigan. When Steve walks into the gym or onto the field, a smile crosses the faces of the coaches, knowing the game will be well managed by Steve and his crew.

Starting out at the age of 12 umpiring PeeWee baseball, his talents have led him to officiate in many of Michigan's major sporting establishments such as, Tiger Stadium, Comerica Park, Pontiac Silverdome, Ford Field, The Palace of Auburn Hills, Breslin Center, Spartan Stadium, Chrysler Arena and the "Big House" of the University of Michigan Wolverines, as well as several other colleges throughout the state. Chances are good that a person attending a high school game from the mid 1980's until early 2016 saw Steve in action. The referee running the entire length of the basketball court with the athletes was most likely Steve Johnson. He prided himself on getting as clear of a sight of the play as the athletes themselves had in order to make a fair call. Football season was no different, running the entire field with the players to make an accurate call on the play.

He gave as much dedication and respect to the game, coaches, and players as he did when he played high school sports.

"These young athletes practice hard, they play hard. They have their blood, sweat, and tears in this sport, they deserve a referee who will work as hard as they do," Steve explains.

He has always loved playing sports, baseball, basketball, football, but baseball was his passion. "I can't remember a time when I wasn't running out of the house to go play ball or playing catch with my brother in the back yard." Like most young boys, Steve's baseball career started with Little League.

In the 1960's, Little League baseball was very popular in Flint. Summer leagues began within days of the school year being finished. Steve and his older brother Butch played baseball all summer long. Steve played left field, catcher, and shortstop.

"I would have played any position the coach asked. I was like all of the other guys, I just wanted to play ball."

The city of Flint had a long history of organized city league baseball beginning in 1909. Prior to the city leagues, Flint was home to several minor league teams. By 1941, the last of five minor league teams to play in Flint's Atwood Stadium were the Flint Arrows. Affiliated with the Cleveland Indians in 1941 as a Class C Michigan State League, they went on to play in the Class A Central League from 1948 – 1951 for the Detroit Tigers.

In the 1960's, the city leagues became so popular in Flint that two divisions, East and West, had to be created to accommodate the number of players. Baseball was an important summer activity to kids and their families in Flint, Michigan. For most people at this time, baseball mitts were the favorite Christmas present and summer became synonymous with baseball. To this day, a local car dealership, Applegate Chevrolet continues to run an ad with the jingle,

"Baseball, hot dogs, Applegate and Chevrolet...sure sounds like Flint to me!"

This was the city in which Steve Johnson grew up playing baseball.

In high school, he and Butch were teammates on the varsity baseball team for the Carman Cougars High School in Flint for one year before Butch graduated. Other than the high school, they liked participating on the same teams. While they both played several positions, often Butch pitched, and Steve played catcher.

"We thought we were untouchable, Butch and I. I'd raze the batter, trying to psych him out." Steve laughs at the memory.

About this time Steve started flirting with the idea of going further with his baseball career. He knew the game. He loved everything about the game, the smell of the leather glove, the crack of the bat making contact with the ball as the sweat trickled down his back. He would not be the first young man who believed that he had the goods for the next level league.

After high school, Steve continued to play city league ball. Mullin's Sporting Goods sponsored the team for which Steve played. Reminiscing about those years Steve says, "We were the worst team in the league! We did win some we weren't supposed to win. We looked forward to spending the evening on the baseball field after a day of working. We just loved playing!" Some of these men had been high school rivals, but now they were family sharing a common passion, the game of baseball.

In 1971, at nineteen years old, Steve was invited to play in the summer league All-Star game: Flint City All Stars vs. Saginaw All Stars. He played left field and was the lead off hitter, the person who bats first. Here was the opportunity he was dreaming about. Knowing that the possibility of scouts being in the audience was great, he planned to show them and the fans what he was capable of doing on the baseball field. He believed he was ready.

His first time at bat he faced pitcher Lary Sorenson. Lary had a reputation of being a good pitcher and rumor was that he was being scouted by the majors. Sorenson ultimately was drafted by the Milwaukee Brewers. He had talent. Lary threw Steve three curveballs which were faster than any fast balls he had ever faced.

"I don't think I ever saw the ball. He made me look silly. I thought I was a pretty good hitter, but when I saw what pro pitchers gave...I knew I wasn't going pro." That is when coaching and officiating became his future. He still loved the game and wanted to continue to be a part of it. For Steve, the next level would be a career of officiating which would last over 40 years.

During his career as an official he would officiate 14 state finals in boys' high school football, baseball, and both girls' and boys' basketball. He also officiated several quarter final and semi-finals in all four sports and spent many years officiating junior college basketball and college baseball.

In March 2004, with a record-breaking crowd of 14,750 fans, he had the honor of officiating the only sellout crowd in the history of MHSSA Basketball Tournament at Michigan State's Breslin Center.

Steve Johnson, Tony Payne (deceased), Mike Knabusch

Steve was born in 1952 in Flint, Michigan, the third child of Walter and Billie Marie Johnson. As a young boy, Steve and his brother Butch worked at their dad's gas station, Johnson's Auto Service. As soon as their dad felt they were old enough, they were pumping gas and washing windshields.

"Working for dad sucked! Hours were long and the pay was bad," Steve laughs, "We lived in a time when asking for a paycheck from our old man got us the, 'Are you ready to pay for room and board' speech or worse yet, the look that told us we had better leave the room fast! Dad gave us money when we really needed it, but you better believe we earned it."

Steve was brought up in a typical 1950's working class household. His father worked while his mother stayed home taking care of the children and having a clean home with dinner on the table when dad returned in the evening. Then church on Sundays. Steve and his siblings attended catechism until seventh grade at St. Luke's Catholic Church in Flint.

"Once I left home, I only attended church if I had to for weddings or something like that. I didn't quit church for any reason other than I wasn't told I had to be there. I was playing sports, working, and hanging out with my friends. I guess I just got out of the habit."

By the time Steve was sixteen, his father sold the auto station. Immediately, Steve started delivering newspapers, pushing an ice cream chart in the neighborhood and selling candy to earn money. From those jobs he got hired in at Arlen's Department Store in the camera department. He worked for Arlen's for a couple of years until he graduated from high school. Then he and his buddy, Woody followed the trend of most young kids fresh out of high school during this time in Flint's history and got hired into General Motors, or "the shop" as locals called it.

Flint became the birthplace of General Motors in 1908. William "Billy" Durant got the idea to combine several small car companies, such as Buick and Olds Motor Works (Oldsmobile) in an effort to be more competitive and profitable. Flint went from being known as "Carriage Town" to "The Vehicle City". The carriage manufacturing town grew from 1,300 residents in 1900 to 91,000 in 1920. By the 1950's the majority of children in school had at least one parent employed by General Motors.

During the years when Steve was a young man was a time in Flint when kids who did not go to college had two options: Work for General Motors in the car factory or get the hell out of town. While Steve did ultimately choose the latter, he along with several other men and woman worked in the shop.

The first day he walked into the factory he thought to himself, 'this is not for me'. It was dark, stuffy, and noisy. The small dirty windows allowed for little sunshine to enter and absolutely no fresh air. The work was physically demanding and dangerous. While Steve wasn't afraid to work, he found himself in an entirely new atmosphere which felt more oppressive than an opportunity.

These men and women were not interested in making friends, and they certainly weren't there to laugh at jokes or share funny stories. Talking to someone could break their concentration, which could result in the loss of a finger or at the very least, stitches. Besides, it was too noisy and hot to carry on a decent conversation. Men and women were there to put in their 30 years to pay mortgages, send kids to college and hopefully live long enough to retire with a pension. Very few of the assembly line workers wanted this lifestyle for their own children. The demanding jobs were a means to an end, to create a better life for their families. It was good pay and offered good benefits such as health insurance for their family, and a pension in return for their labors.

Steve wasn't alone when he says that he dreaded going into the factory every day. His second week on the job, he was assigned to the fender line. Heavy metal fenders were suspended overhead from a moving assembly line. As the part was approaching, the line-worker had to pull the auto part down and place it on the vehicle. They used every part of their bodies to fit their assigned part onto the car. After grabbing the fender, Steve would use his knee to hold it into place while using the air gun to attach it to the vehicle. As soon as he finished one fender, he had to be prepared to reach up for the next one. The assembly line moved swiftly and so did the autoworkers. Unfamiliar with his new assigned environment, a fender quickly came down the line and instead of Steve grabbing it, it grabbed him. Momentarily stunned, his first thought was he was too young to lose an arm or suffer a permanent eye injury. It came awfully close to his face. It scared him. He knew right then and there, that was his last day. He finished out his shift and immediately began looking for another source of employment.

After his short time with General Motors he worked for Pepsi Cola delivering to local businesses. Driving a semi - truck, he was could see the sun, breathe in cool air, and interact with people. Even on the worse weather days, driving through snowstorms and ice, he was much happier than he had been the short time he worked for General Motors. When he lost his two front teeth when a pallet of cans fell from the truck and one lone can smacked him in the mouth, he was happier than working at the shop. Two years later, sugar prices soared and being low man on the totem pole of employees, Steve was laid off from Pepsi.

During that period of time, his sole means of income was from officiating. A job he loved.

A few days later, as if an answer to his employment dilemma, a high school friend contacted him from Las Vegas. He told Steve that his dad managed a small hotel in Las Vegas called the Orbit Inn, and they were looking for dealers. They offered Steve free dealer training if he wanted the job. Steve heard the call, 'Go West Young Man' and decided it was time to leave Flint. He and Terri decided it was time to set a wedding date and begin their life together in Nevada.

Steve and Terri Johnson 1978

Arriving in Las Vegas as newlyweds, Steve and Terri were excited to start the beginning of their lives together. Steve spent 30 days at the Orbit Inn. During this time, he learned to deal Blackjack, Roulette, Craps, and the duties required of a Pit Boss. Once the training was completed, he set out to find a better paying job. Immediately hired after his Friday audition, Monday he began his new position as a dealer for The Golden Nugget Casino and Hotel. It wasn't long before he realized that each casino had a softball team which played against other casinos and the Las Vegas Police Team. 2,005 miles from home and baseball found its way back into Steve's life.

For three years, Steve worked and played softball for the Golden Nugget and the team only won one game, but he was playing ball and that was all that mattered. Once again, Steve found himself with a group of men who became a family both on and off the field. Eventually, University of Las Vegas basketball player, Flint Ray Williams joined the team. He played first base and Steve played shortstop, however both men tried to play the entire field. As with the other players, they were all there to have fun playing a game they all loved, softball.

The last game of the season, Mike Howard, casino manager at The Golden Nugget approached Steve. Mike was leaving for The Tropicana Hotel and Casino and wanted Steve to join him...Monday. Not only was this a promotion for Mike, but a huge one for Steve as well. Steve always brought in good tips, but the Tropicana had an entirely different clientele. Within the first week his tips increased by $50.00 to $120.00 a day.

Within a few days of working at The Tropicana he was approached by team pitcher, Tony Barilla. Knowing that

Steve had played ball for The Golden Nugget, Tony invited Steve to play on his team with The Tropicana. Steve was asked what position he wanted to play to which Steve replied, "Shortstop". Tony informed Steve that their team didn't need a player for that position, it was already filled. Steve shrugged his shoulders and repeated, "I play shortstop." Instead of arguing Tony invited Steve to come to a practice and see how he fit in with the team. Not committing to join the team, Steve did attend a practice.

"Truthfully, I would have played whatever position they had available. I was that guy who had a need in my bones to play ball. I just liked shortstop; I was really good and confident in that position."

Before the next game, Monday night, The Tropicana had a new shortstop. They also had a new third base player, the previous shortstop. Steve recalls that the team was made up of a great group of guys. With the addition of Steve, all positions played were solidly covered and The Tropicana became the team to beat. The team played well together, both on and off the field.

The Tropicana made it to the league championship.

"We were competitive, but we also had fun! Everyone of us loved the game, some more than others," Steve chuckles at the memory, "When we made it to the play offs and found ourselves facing the Las Vegas Metropolitan Police team we were determined that they weren't going to hand us our asses. We were going to play hard and party *after* the game!" Steve laughs at the memory and then goes into sportscaster mode. "I'll never forget that game as long as I live. I can still see it as if it were yesterday. It was the bottom of the seventh inning with the score tied, 6-6. We knew we were a good team, but the police team was better. We had a man on second with two outs. I was up to bat. My biggest worry at that moment was to not strike out. I didn't want to be *that* guy. You never live that down no matter how many things you have done right! The pitch came and I hit a double down the left field line to knock in the winning run! We won the championship, dethroning the police team! It was a tremendous win for The Tropicana and for the team." Chuckling he adds, "Of course, after that game we had to watch our p's and q's while driving around town!"

Steve was in his glory! He and his wife were expecting their first child, he had a job he enjoyed, and he was playing softball with a great group of guys.

The ten years Steve and Terri lived in Las Vegas they had many great experiences, made many friends and started a family. Both their sons, Brad (1982) and Bryan (1984) were born in Vegas. While working as a dealer, Steve met many people from all walks of life including sports celebrities. He even had an Arab Sheik who would ask specifically for Steve to deal when he visited Las Vegas. His expectations were that Steve would follow him from game to game, wherever he went. With a shudder, Steve recalls,

"You have no idea how stressful that was. He would bet large sums, upwards of a million dollars in an eight-hour shift. I couldn't even have a break until he wanted one! But not matter if he won or lost, he'd always tip me ten thousand dollars, so of course I never complained!"

On May 17, 1985 he became the first person to deal in the Million Dollar Blackjack Tournament at the Tropicana.

"Now that was a very tense event. The Blackjack table was moved into the casino theater and set up on a stage. There were camera crews everywhere, filming every angle to broadcast it throughout the Vegas area. It was amazing."

Apparently, Steve wasn't the only one who thought the event went well. Casino manager, Toby di Casare sent a letter in which he credits Steve with "the professional manner in which you conducted yourself in a very tense situation" Mr. Di Casare also goes on to say that he also, "made it possible for our guests to enjoy the Tropicana Hotel's special interest in service and courtesy." To this day, this letter is framed and proudly displayed in his 'man cave' located in the basement of his house. "I don't believe my wife feels it goes well with the décor of the living room, so it is on my wall of awards," Steve jokes.

Letter from Toby di Casare

Along with his duties as a pit boss, Steve also wrote a sports column called, "Sports Scene" for the "Talk of the Trop" casino newspaper as well as a sports column for "The Tourist, Industry, People News" which was distributed throughout the Las Vegas area. This was a dream job for Steve. He had access to sporting events and athletes. As if that weren't enough, he was asked to write about something he loved, sports.

"I often would read other sports columnist and think that I would have focused on a different aspect of the game. A few times I even wondered if they had watched the same game I did! Suddenly, I had the opportunity and I ran with it. Interviewing celebrity athletes was just as exciting for me as talking with other casino employees about sports, any sports. It didn't matter what sport we were talking about."

While Steve enjoyed interviewing several sporting greats, his most memorable were with two legendary players, boxer Ray 'Boom-Boom' Mancini and golfer Payne Stewart.

"Both interviews I had to really work hard to get," Steve recalls. With Boom-Boom, every time I went to the ring to try to get an interview, he was unavailable, or I had just missed him. I was getting desperate. This was going to be a big fight and I needed this interview. Finally, I was able to get his room number and went up and just introduced myself. I spent an hour and a half interviewing him on everything from the upcoming match to our opinions on other sports. He was a real easy guy to talk with." Steve was told later that Mancini has never before allowed an interview in his hotel room.

"I guess I just got lucky," Steve says with a laugh.

Article of "Boom-Boom Mancini framed on Steve's wall

As Steve begins to talk about his interview with the late Payne Smith his demeanor changes. No longer is his voice charged with excitement and momentarily the sparkle in his eye is replaced with sadness.

"Man, I'll never forget watching as that plane flew on auto-pilot. I kept thinking what a tragedy this was, the guy was so full of life, he was young and had small children. I really admired his style. He was had a smooth swing and great golfing outfits. He always wore bright colored knickers and a tam on his head. It was so cool," Steve shakes his head sadly before he continues as if he's giving Payne a moment of respectful silence at his memory. "It was another one of those interviews that I was struggling to get. I couldn't ever seem to be at the right place at the right time. Then I heard that he was going to do an early practice, I think it was at 6:30 in the morning. It was much earlier than I was up, but I wanted to meet this guy. I had a lot of admiration for him. This interview was one of the few where I was a little starstruck. So, I got my butt out of bed and went down to where he was practicing. He was very gracious with me, even though I was interrupting his practice. I still get chills when I think about that plane flying on autopilot for hours with everyone on board dead."

When asked which memory stands out more for him than others Steve doesn't talk about the celebrities or the rich and famous, he talks about "the greatest hand of all time". He was dealing Blackjack at The Golden Nugget with eight decks of cards to six people.

"It was wild! Every player had a blackjack and I had an ace showing. I offered each player the chance to buy insurance, no one took it." Insurance for blackjack is a protection for your hand. Should the dealer have an ace showing insurance is offered, it is the only time it is offered. The cost to the player is half of their bet. Taking the insurance offers you 2 to 1 on your bet against the dealer also having blackjack.

"I offered the insurance a second time with the same answer...no. I was as shock as everyone else when I turned up a king giving me a blackjack as well. I couldn't believe it! Nobody got paid."

Despite all their adventures, the glitz and glamour of Las Vegas, by 1986 it was time for the Johnsons to go home.

Steve and Terri were both raised in the Flint area, and their parents still lived there. The boys were 2 and 4 years old when they decided it was time to return home to Flint, Michigan. In Vegas they had many close friends, but family was in the Midwest. They still tell people that Vegas was a great place, but they wanted to raise their boys in a different environment. The environment they had both enjoyed, surrounded by family. Flint was home. Within a very short time of returning home Steve was back to referring games. A passion he has had since he was a young boy.

*let us therefore come boldly unto the throne
of grace, that we may obtain mercy, and
find grace to help in time of need.*

Hebrews 4:16

Chapter Two

The day Steve and Terri got their diagnosis was a day that would forever change their lives, as well as that of their family and a group of people Steve would refer to his personal "Prayer Warriors".

The week started out as all his weeks did. At 62, he still worked full time with his brother Butch during the day and in the evenings, he officiated high school sports. He also owned a traveling casino entertainment business, with his buddy Pat Doyle, called Las Vegas Knights. Weekends and holidays, they traveled with their tables and roulette wheel to deal cards and entertain at private parties. These events consisted of loading and unloading a 350-pound Craps Table, a Blackjack table weighing 110 pounds, several 60-pound Poker Tables as well as assorted chips and other paraphernalia. After the set up it was show time! Steve resumed his previous Vegas position of Pit Boss and became the personality of the party.

Typically, during these events he would mingle with the crowd, tell a few jokes, share a funny tidbit, and on occasion was known to sing-along on stage with the band.

Then in the wee hours of the morning he and Pat would load up and drive home. Often times this was all done after spending a full day working with his brother.

Pat Doyle and Steve Johnson (left) Terri Johnson (right)

On this particular night, after officiating a high school baseball game where temperatures soared to the 100-degree mark, he did something he had never done. As soon as the equipment was unloaded, he crawled into his utility van and took a nap. He was drained of energy and just needed to sleep. He figured a few moments of rest and he'd be just fine. Instead of working the floor and mingling with the guests he simply walked around and watched the others. This evening he was only there should his crew need a bathroom break, or if one of the tables needed attention. He was not feeling like his usual gregarious self.

His wife had been encouraging him to go see a doctor all month, his constant fatigue wasn't normal for him. He repeatedly reminded her that he'd just had a sports physical, which he did yearly as a referee, and had gotten a clean bill of health. His younger sister, Sherry and her husband Dave worked the Vegas Knights' party that evening, they wanted him to go to the Emergency Room that night. Steve was too tired to argue and truthfully, he wanted this fatigue to end. He was tired of being tired. He agreed he would call his doctor for an appointment...tomorrow. However, he believed that all he needed was to catch up on his sleep. He was sure that tomorrow or at the latest next week he would feel better. He was feeling exhaustion long before Friday's party, but he still pushed himself, he had work to do.

The next day he was scheduled to golf in the Tom Cole Memorial Scramble, which is an annual fund-raising event to promote and sponsor Flint baseball. Steve and his brother Butch have participated in this event from the beginning. Depending on which of their sons were available determined who played on their team, sometimes it was only one of their sons and one of their friends. Steve was also scheduled to be the Master of Ceremony (MC) for the auction after the event was finished.

The next morning, he was still feeling tired. For the first time in years, he really didn't want to go golfing with his family and life-long friends and even considered canceling, but he also didn't want to let the guys down nor miss helping in a cause in which he believed...Flint Baseball.

As he got to the golf course, he started feeling the exhaustion coming over him in waves. He did not feel like his usual exuberant self. He wanted to find somewhere to take a nap. With his brother driving the golf cart, Steve participated in the tournament. "I golfed, if you want to call what I was doing golfing!" After each swing of the club, he would crawl back in the cart and close his eyes. It was still early in the morning, and already the temperatures were proving that it was going to be another scorcher. "I kept thinking that if I could just get a couple minutes of sleep, I'd be fine." That was not the case.

After his team completed the Scramble, he made his apologies to his team and the group. He did not feel well enough to perform as auctioneer. He was going home to go back to bed. His agenda was cleared due to the tournament and he was going to use this time to catch up on his sleep.

When he walked in the house his wife was surprised to see him home so early. He told her he was too tired to golf and just wanted to go to bed. Perhaps, he explained, he had caught a virus, or a summer flu. As he pulled off his shirt to take a shower before his nap, his wife took one look at him and said, "No more waiting. We're going to the doctor NOW!" What she saw sent a shockwave of fear through her body. He had lost 15 pounds from his usually fit 150-pound frame and had never shown this level of fatigue in his life. His bones were protruding through his back, he didn't have an ounce of meat on his bones. Terri knew immediately something more than a virus was causing her husband's fatigue and weight loss, he was sicker than either of them thought.

"I could count the individual bones in his spine and each rib. I couldn't believe what I was seeing. It was like those pictures you see of Holocaust victims. I knew it was much more serious than the flu." Terri recalls with a shudder.

Steve(left) and Butch (brother) Johnson

Earlier that winter, even though he was tired, Steve decided their house needed repainted.

"I was planning to do inside things until the weather changed so that I could spend my time outside when the weather was nice again. I knew that if I waited until winter was over it would be another year before the house got painted." But he was still tired. "I couldn't sleep. The things that I wanted to complete were making me anxious. I'd lay down and think, just finish that wall and then call it a night."

Still working full time and refereeing, along with his home beautification, were the excuses he used to explain away his exhaustion. He started being too tired to eat. By the time his entire three-bedroom ranch home was completely repainted, his garage and shed were purged of years of storing things, it was summer, and he was still constantly tired.

The weeks prior to his diagnosis was unseasonably hot. In Michigan, 100-degree weather usually doesn't begin until the end of June, first of July. July's temperatures arrived a month early the summer of 2016, but Steve still worked in his yard, mowing and trimming. When it was this hot, he'd work for 20 minutes, get a drink, then drench himself with the garden hose before returning to his yard work until it was finished. He had a great amount of pride in his yard and the vegetable garden he and his wife always planted.

Terri had already planted the garden in May, before her husband's diagnosis. Usually their vegetable garden was an enormous amount of work, but the yield was plentiful and well worth the effort. Steve always loved grilling their vegetables and sharing them with the neighbors. As their garden began maturing, he would start counting down the days until he could make a fresh tomato sandwich. He'd tell people, "There is nothing like biting into a tomato that tastes like a tomato." This year, as the garden matured, Steve was too ill to eat any of the vegetables he had always loved.

This summer he wasn't as motivated to get out in the yard and garden. "I was tired. I just wanted to sleep. I kept telling myself it'll be cooler tomorrow; I'll do it then." Even though fatigue plagued his every waking moment, he was not the type of person to sit back and watch the grass grow. He had to do something active. Prior to his diagnosis, he decided to build a Disc Golf Course. He got the idea after playing during a cookout at his son Bryan's house. At first, he was just going to build one from the items he had from cleaning out his garage. He used the top of a grill and some pieces of old chain and attached it to a 2 ½ foot pipe with a 2 ½" pvc cap. After he built the first one, he started a second and then a third.

As he was building them, he started designing theme holes. He envisioned that the first hole, naturally was to be his favorite college team, Michigan State. His green and white decorated hole even proudly displayed a small garden statue of Sparty, the team mascot. To be fair to his University of Michigan friends, his next hole was blue and gold, he even added a scarlet and gray Ohio State hole. Chuckling to himself, he imagined the good-natured razzing he and his friends would have over these three holes alone.

Quickly he decided to create an entire course, each hole would have a theme. The longest hole would be 145 yards, with 40 yards being the shortest. Excited, he began planning a Father's Day barbecue party where he would introduce his disc golf course in a couple of weeks. Steve envisioned holding annual Father's Day Tournaments. The teams could be fathers versus sons, or his sons and nephews versus he and his brother. The possibilities were endless.

In addition to his first three holes he was working on adding two holes to represent local high schools where he was a referee and many of his friends once attended, gold and burgundy for Davison High School and a teal one for the newly organized Flint Jaguars. He even had a green and yellow John Deere hole, for his grandson, Brody who loved riding on the John Deere riding lawn mower with his Papa.

Brody's Hole – The John Deere inspired hole.

With three holes built and a fourth one needing a little piece of chain, his exhaustion took over. He was tired. Father's Day was still a couple days away. He told himself he'd run to the hardware store for the last part...tomorrow. Right now, he wanted a nap.

He had painted his entire house throughout the winter and had cleaned out his garage getting rid of things he didn't even remember he had, worked in his yard, created a Disc Golf Course, now he wanted to take on day for himself and relax. He had time tomorrow. He told himself that he didn't have to do it all in one week. He believed he had time, he just needed to rest. This was his belief until he sat in the doctor's office two days prior to Father's Day.

Two weeks prior to sitting in the doctor's waiting room with his wife, he had already decided that his exhaustion was his body's way of telling him to act his age. It was time to retire from the full-time position with his brother's company. He was at the age where he could collect Social Security plus, he still had his entertainment company, Las Vegas Knights along with his refereeing, two things he loved doing. Little did he know that those two things would also come to a screeching halt.

That day at the doctor's office a chest x-ray was ordered. Steve started feeling a little relieved, he probably had pneumonia. That would explain his constant fatigue. That, and grinning to himself, his age. He would let his brother know that he was going to quit working and after baseball season it would be time to start enjoying his golden years with his wife and family.

Sadly, pneumonia wasn't the doctor's diagnosis. The doctor came in and explained to Steve and Terri that he wasn't happy with the x-ray.

"When the doctor walked in the room and told us that he was concerned about the x-ray and that he made an appointment for us to see an oncologist and a pulmonologist I couldn't believe my ears. I knew Steve was sick, but not THAT sick. I was scared."
Terri recalls. Adding to his wife's statement Steve holds up his fist, "There was a mass the size of my fist in my chest!"

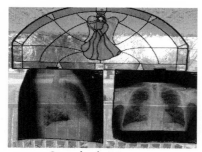
Steve's chest x-rays

The very next day, with his wife by his side, Steve went through a series of tests. On the inside, the fear of something being seriously wrong began creeping inside of him. On the outside, the technicians and medical personnel saw a man who was confident and full of life.

He was still telling jokes and making others laugh when what he really wanted to do was take a nap.

June 15, 2016, as he and Terri, his wife of 38 years, sat in the pulmonologist's office waiting for the diagnosis, he was trying to be positive. He was going to retire; they were going to start doing the things they had put off doing until later. Later was here, staring him in the face. He prayed for the first time in years, "Lord, please give me something I can fight."

Steve and Terri had plans to travel, he was going to be home more often. They still had friends in Vegas from when they had lived there for almost 10 years. It was past time to go back for a visit and enjoy the town as a tourist, not as residents. If the doctor recommended that he get some rest and take it easy for a while, he was going to do that immediately, no ifs, ands, or buts. He was already formulating his plan as they sat in there waiting for the doctor.

He began picturing their travel plans in his mind. It was going to be hot in Vegas, but he was going to visit old friends, visit the casinos, catch a show. They weren't going to be outside in the heat, they would be inside where the air conditioners gave the illusion of a temperate climate. The town came alive at night. He would sit at the tables he used to work, compare notes with the new guy and tell stories about his years as a casino dealer. He would even bring a few pictures to show while he was there. Closing his eyes, he started to relax. He had a plan.

Abruptly, the pulmonologist came in and thrust the x-ray Steve and Terri brought from their family doctor on the lightboard, pointed to a mass the size of his fist and without preamble asked, "Do you have a will?" Stunned, unable to breath, all Steve could think was, "Hell, yes I have a will! A will to live!"

The pulmonologist continued with her death sentence, "You have small cell lung cancer." As the doctor droned on about his imminent demise, thoughts of Vegas vanished, and he began thinking about all he was going to lose. His new baby grandson Brody was just starting to walk. He would never be able to throw him a baseball or watch him play in a game. At a year old, Brody would grow up not remembering Steve. His beautiful granddaughter Katelyn was growing up so fast. She had just started playing volleyball in middle school. He wouldn't be there to see her drive, go to prom, or graduate.

He looked around the room and couldn't believe that he was actually here. He could hear his wife talking to the doctor but had no idea what either of them were saying.

"It all felt like I was watching someone else's life, not mine. This can't be happening to me. It felt like I was having an out of body experience. I could see everything but was unable to participate. I was in a fog."

As they sat there in stunned silence, they learned that small cell cancer is a very aggressive cancer. It grows rapidly and spreads quickly to other parts of the body. His cancer was advanced. Of the five stages of cancer, Steve was in Stage 4 and it had traveled to his bones. Muscle weakness, fatigue, loss of appetite and weight loss were not from being an extremely active 62-year-old man working in the excessive heat. They were the symptoms of small cell lung cancer.

The doctor continued to tell them that Steve had a mass in his lungs and one on his windpipe. Terri recalls feeling like the blood was draining from her body, "If I was asked to stand up, I think I would have fallen." Before she could catch her breath, the doctor informed her that the mass on his windpipe could kill Steve at any minute. His heart would stop, and he would die in his sleep. Frightened, Terri asked what she should do if that happens. She was told flatly, "Nothing. They won't be able to bring him back."

Leaving the doctor's office in a daze, both he and his wife had more questions than answers. Were they supposed to follow the pulmonologist advice, get their affairs in order, lie back and wait to die? She had given Steve 2 – 3 months to live. Would he be alive to celebrate Christmas, or would his family be attending his funeral? Where were they supposed to start? What was the next step?

Terri and Steve had two sons, Brad and Bryan, his brother and sister, Butch and Sherry, his sister-in-law Liz, nieces and nephews, not to mention close friends. Was he supposed to call them up individually? Invite them over for dinner and make an announcement over dessert? What about treatment? According to the doctor, he might be able to stretch his time to 3-6 months with chemotherapy. This cancer was aggressive and incurable. He kept thinking, "Why bother going through treatment if it wasn't going to change anything?" He might squeak out another month or two, but at what quality of life? Through all these questions, he still didn't feel like this was him they were talking about. He just kept thinking, "This can't be the end. I'm not afraid to die. I'm just not ready to die." It was all surreal.

Looking back, the changes in Steve weren't as subtle as it seemed to those who knew him. His brother Butch commented on the fact that Steve never used to fall asleep in the car.

"We'd go to a job and the car would be filled with four or five guys and Steve would have everyone laughing at his stories. It seemed like all of a sudden he was taking naps during the car rides, both there and back."

"He would come home after working, take a shower and nap before he left to officiating a game, then come home and fall asleep on the couch. He was always too tired to eat, or he'd fall asleep before he would decide what he wanted to eat." His wife recalls.

Even Steve himself mentioned how he never really felt quite like himself. Family parties or dinner with friends became a chore instead of an event he looked forward to attending. He worked all day and wanted to stay home.

Steve would be the first to tell you that he was rich – rich in his relationships with friends and family. He would soon discover over the next few months how rich those relationships were. When news of his illness reached his loved ones, they all reached out to him. People he saw or spoke to daily as well as people he hadn't seen in years reached out to him and his family. He knew he had their love and support. What he was coming to realize was that what he didn't have was time.

But we see Jesus, who was made a little lower than the angels for the suffering of death, crowned with glory and honour; that he by the grace of God should taste death for every man.
Hebrew 2:9

Chapter Three

Less than 50 years ago a cancer diagnosis was basically a death sentence with only two options; chemotherapy or radiation. Victims could almost count on suffering from hair loss and constant vomiting along with the deep seeded dread that their days were numbered. Advancements in modern medicine, alternative treatments and improved living conditions are creating more success stories of surviving cancer than ever before.

After leaving the doctor's office that June afternoon, stunned and feeling lost, he decided not to go through with the trouble of chemotherapy both for himself and his family. He was told it was hopeless, why bother being miserable for the few remaining months he had left. He was given a two to three-month life span, 60 to 90 days, he decided that he was going to live everyday to the fullest. He was going to make memories with the people he loved. He wouldn't see Katelyn go to her first dance, graduate, or watch his youngest son walk her down the aisle. He needed to let her know that he would be watching; even though his physical body was absent, his love and spirit would always be with her. His baby grandson wouldn't remember riding around the yard on the riding mower with him even when the grass didn't need to be cut, but their story would live on in pictures and videos. He had the need to make sure that both Katelyn and Brody knew that their Papa adored them. He and his wife had a close and loving relationship, he wanted to make sure she knew that she was the best thing that ever happened to him. He had a couple short months to make up for all the long hours he worked, the retirement promises which were being broken and the sorrow his passing would impose upon her.

We all know we are going to die. In the circle of life, one expects to outlive their parents. When one marries, they know there is a fifty percent chance that they will outlive their spouse. This is the way of life, people expect it. The moment a person is born, they are one second closer to death. Fortunately, most people do not dwell on that fact throughout their lives. As a kid, being 30 was, "so old". The first benchmark children are anxious to reach is the age where they can stay up past 9:30 on a weeknight. Then they want to be 16 and get their driver's license, 18 so that they can leave home and be their own boss. At that point they are just anxious to live their 20's to the fullest. Once they become 30, the new "old age" is 50, then 75 and 80 years old and they have found a new appreciation for the naps they once fought against decades earlier.

With today's medical advances and understanding of a healthy lifestyle, it isn't unreasonable to believe a person will live to become 90 or even 100 years old. The saddest part of this knowledge is that too often individuals put off things because they believe they will have time.

Steve was at a point in his life where he truly believed he had another 25 or 30 good years, at least. He was healthy, active and loved his life. He had held some exciting jobs, met some interesting people, and had a large loving network of family and friends. Being told that it was abruptly coming to an end in a matter of weeks was something he couldn't even wrap his mind around. Trying to be brave as he told everyone the love he had for them was excruciatingly hard, not because he wasn't used to telling people that he loved them, but because it might be the last time they hear it from him and he needed to make sure they felt the depth of his feelings. There were a lot of tears, a lot of feelings of injustice, and a lot of people who wanted to help him fight. Steve just didn't see the point of going through chemo or radiation just to prolong his life another month or two, especially knowing that his quality of life would be compromised with being sick the entire time. He didn't want pity or sympathy; he was tired but wanted to enjoy the little bit of time he had left with those he loved.

Needless to say, his wife Terri was scared.

"I've lived with him for most of my life and now I'm being told I have to say good-bye. I don't know how to live without him."

They were at a point in their lives where they were both retired. He promised that they were going to travel and do the things they been too busy to do while raising kids and earning a living. He told her that he was going to be home more often, instead of working crazy long hours, leaving before dawn, coming home to shower and change clothes to referee a game, then returning home well after dark. Finally, they were going to start doing all the things they had planned and dreamed about. Now Terri was faced with the emptiness of him not being there to share.

Steve had always been in tip-top shape from the day she met him at a Flint Generals Hockey Game. While they dated, he played softball and officiated games at least twice a week. Smiling at the memory, Terri recalls a promotional ad ran by the Tropicana Casino featuring Steve dealing cards shirtless. "He's always been so active and fit. That ad was a big hit!"

Steve Johnson

Their boys were grown with families of their own. It was going to be just Steve and Terri again for the first time since their oldest son, Brad was born in 1982. Instead of planning their golden years, she and her husband of thirty-eight years were being asked if they had a will.

As Steve's weight rapidly decreased, Terri watched their dreams dwindled away before her eyes. She was scared...and tired. Being strong for someone you love while you're falling apart is exhausting. Watching death slowly taking the person you have structured most of your adult years with is excruciating. Every emotion she felt had to be hidden behind a brave smile, as she couldn't let him know how truly frightened, she was of losing him. She never complained nor did she cry in front of Steve.

And without faith it is impossible to please God,
because anyone who comes to him must believe
that he exists and that he rewards those who
earnestly.

Hebrews 11:6

Chapter Four

When their sons got old enough Steve coached their Little League Baseball Team for a couple of years.

"They may have been my boys, but I worked very hard to treat them as I did all of the other boys on the team. I taught all of those boys to love the game, to respect the other team, and above all to have fun."

Coach Steve (left) Bryan and Brad(right) Johnson

Both their boys, like their father, enjoyed sports and were active in many high school sports. Brad wrestled and golfed while Bryan was more active in baseball and football. Being a high school referee, it was only a matter of time before Steve would find himself officiating one of Bryan's games. One game in particular stands out most in both Steve and Terri's memories. Bryan was playing 9th grade baseball and his dad was not only officiating the game but was the umpire. Bryan came up to bat, standing poised to hit the ball as his dad took his position behind him.

"Bryan struck out. I had no choice but to call it a strike. He never took a swing. All three balls were strike balls." Striking out in front of your teammates was bad enough, but having you own father call you out was horrible. A few parents in the stands who knew that the batter was Steve's son were probably even more surprised, expecting some form of nepotism.

"I'll never forget how he glared at me when I called him out! I looked right back at him and said, 'maybe next time you'll swing at the ball.' That didn't go over well at all! He didn't speak to me for an entire week," Steve laughs.

Over the years officiating and playing baseball, Steve made many lasting and deep friendships. One of his closest friends is Flint Judge Duncan Beagle. Steve and Duncan met while playing on a summer baseball league after high school. Quickly, both young men realized they shared a common passion, the love of baseball. It didn't matter if they were watching or playing, baseball was as necessary to them as oxygen. It wasn't about winning, it was about playing and being a part of something good and wholesome. They both found themselves on a team sponsored by Mullin's Sporting Goods. According to Steve, they had a lot of fun playing, and the team became very close, but they were the worst team on the league.

Playing league ball wasn't enough for either of them. During this time, they both decided to begin officiating for high school sporting events. They became friends on the field as well as off and remained in close contact with one another during the years Steve lived in Las Vegas. Little did either of them know that this friendship would literally save both of their lives one day.

Many years later, while officiating a basketball game, Duncan, then a lawyer in Flint started feeling a weakness in his legs while on the court. He had been experiencing episodes of tingling numbness in his legs throughout the past few days. He was a little surprised when the numbness began happening even while he was being active. More than once he felt like he was going to collapse. There were not any other symptoms accompanying this numbness and it seemed to come and go. He tried to pass off the numbing sensation from sitting too long or possibly a pinch nerve. Then came the day when he simply couldn't stand and support his own weight. This was serious, it was evident that is was past time to go see a doctor. Duncan was immediately taken to the hospital.

When Steve heard that his longtime friend and fellow referee was in the hospital, he immediately went to the hospital to offer his support. When Steve arrived at the hospital, he recalls feeling like he had walked into a funeral parlor. The room was dark, and the atmosphere was heavy with despair. The melancholy reception Steve got from Duncan was not typical, the warmth in his voice and the light in his eyes were missing. Duncan was despondent and told Steve that he didn't feel up to having any visitors. Steve, in typical fashion, immediately began telling jokes and putting his familiar humorous spin on stories of the day. As if Duncan had not spoken, Steve did not heed his request and made sure he visited Duncan daily.

Years later, Duncan would say that Steve made him laugh when all he wanted to do was let the darkness envelope him and be divorced from the world.

Steve visited Duncan every day while he was in the hospital, and when the diagnosis came in, Steve was there to help him through. Duncan was diagnosed with Guillain-Barre Syndrome and would spend the rest of his life confined to a wheelchair.

Guillain-Barre Syndrome is when the immune system attacks the peripheral nervous system. These are the group of nerves which run from the brain down the spinal cord. Nerves are protected by a type of insulator, much like electrical wires, called myelin. A healthy immune system will attack viruses and foreign invaders to prevent illnesses. Guillain-Barre Syndrome does the opposite, it attacks the healthy myelin covering the nerves. This prevents the signals from the brain being received by the person's arms and legs. The symptoms are pins and needle numbness leading to complete paralysis. In extreme cases it will affect the lungs and cause death. The disease is rare and has no known cure.

Duncan was at the top of his game both personally and professionally. He had recently been appointed circuit court judge by Michigan Governor John Engler. He also had recently asked his girlfriend to marry him. Lying in the hospital bed unable to move his own legs, he began to wonder how fair it was to ask his fiancée' to start a new life with a man confined to a wheelchair.

Steve continued to visit Duncan every day, while Dana rarely left Duncan's bedside. Neither Dana nor Steve were willing to allow Duncan to slip into a dark cloud of despair; they weren't giving up on Duncan and they weren't going to let him give up either. Steve would find out 26 years later how much his friendship saved Duncan and Dana Beagle's lives and ultimately his own.

Dana and Duncan did marry and have a son. A day doesn't pass without the two of them giving thanks to God for the blessings in their lives, and for putting Steve in their presence. The Beagles give credit first to God, and second to Steve. Steve helped Duncan see that throwing himself a pity party was not going to get him anywhere; he needed to be present for this fight. A person with deep faith, Dana continued to look for a way to pay Steve back. She vowed that one day she would find a way to show him how much she appreciated his gift of life that he helped bestow upon Duncan.

Years after being diagnosed with Guillain-Barre Syndrome, the Beagles would discover that he had been misdiagnosed. Despite the number of tests Duncan has endured, the doctors still are not exactly sure what caused his paralysis.

Still believing there was a cure for her husband and having faith in God's miracles, Dana was led to Dr. Issam Nemeh. Dana was in her kitchen when a program on television caught her attention. The television was on, more for background noise than anything else, when Dana heard Dr. Oz introduce his next guest. The Dr. Oz show was featuring a doctor from Ohio who used a faith-based approach to healing. Watching as Dr. Nemeh talked, Dana felt as if she was receiving a direct message to her prayers, a cure for her husband. She located his contact number and made an appointment for her husband to meet Dr. Nemeh at his office in Ohio.

The Beagles have faith that Duncan will walk again one day. This is a belief their good friend Steve Johnson also shares with them.

Steve Johnson and Duncan Beagle

Now faith is the substance of things hoped for,
the evidence of things not seen.
Hebrew 11:1

Chapter Five

As soon as Dana and Duncan learned of Steve's cancer, she told Duncan that they were finally getting the chance to pay their 26-year-old debt to Steve. They were going to take him to see Dr. Nemeh.

When Duncan called Steve the first thing Duncan said to Steve was, "Do you believe in miracles?" Steve was at a low point when he received the call. Prior to the phone call from the Beagles, the oncologist's office had called to schedule an appointment for a biopsy. Steve just wasn't sure he wanted to keep the appointment. He didn't think he could sit in another doctor's office and hear the same diagnosis.

Still in a state of shock and trying to reconcile himself as to how to spend his last moments on earth, he looked over to his wife, shrugged his shoulders and asked her, "What do I have to lose?" Together they decided that the wise decision would be to keep the appointment with the oncologist. At the very least they would know that they didn't just give up without a fighting chance.

Steve had already decided that he didn't want to go through treatments if there was no hope. Being sick for the few precious remaining weeks he had with his family was not how he wanted to be remembered. Nor was it how he wanted to live what was left of his life.

Duncan asked him if he believed in miracles. Weary and frightened, Steve replied, "At this point, my brother, I believe in anything." Duncan then passed the phone to his wife, Dana. Fighting back tears and with a smile in her voice, Dana told Steve that she had waited 26 years to pay him back for saving Duncan. Now it was their turn to save his life. They were going to take him to see Dr. Nemeh.

Listening to Dana speaking about Dr. Nemeh was the beginning of a turning point for Steve. He remembers thinking that he wanted to try anything to avoid dying. He was going to try anything to prolong his life. He had a good life; he enjoyed his life and he wanted it all back. He began feeling a flicker of hope.

"Everything started to come together, it was like God had handed me a written script," Steve says of that phone conversation with the Beagles. With a smile, he adds,

"God has a mind of his own, don't try to read it, because it is impossible. After some of the things that have happened to me, I just can't comprehend it. One thing I have learned with a certainty is that *He* is the only one with the answers and *He* decides when and how to answer."

Steve was learning the age-old lesson many sadly fail to heed, *God's will not mine.* Steve's heart, mind, and soul were opening to God's healing and love.

After the phone call, the Beagles went over to Steve and Terri's home to talk about someone they believed could help. They were going to take Steve to meet Dr. Nemeh, a physician who, in a word, was a spiritual healer as well as a medical doctor. The Johnsons agreed to give it a shot, again at this point, they felt they had nothing to lose. Tired, and fighting through the numbness that engulfed her entire body, Terri called Dr. Nemeh's office to set up an appointment. Unfortunately, she was informed that the doctor was booked for the next few weeks. There wasn't anything available in the immediate future, but they would call if something opened up. Terri wasn't certain that Steve would even have a few weeks left.

Within an hour Dana received a phone call to deliver what they would later realize was the first of many miracles. There was a cancelation. Dr. Nemeh's receptionist wanted to know if the Johnson would be able to drive to Cleveland by noon the next day. Without hesitation, Dana accepted the appointment and made arrange for their 225-mile trip in the morning.

Dana called the Johnsons again later that afternoon to say that Dr. Nemeh wanted a picture of Steve to pray over before he met with him.

The day before he was to meet Dr. Nemeh for the first time Steve had gone for the lung biopsy. After he returned home, he was leaning against a wall in his dining room talking with his youngest son, Bryan. Suddenly Bryan pointed to his dad's chest and asked if he was feeling alright. Looking down, Steve saw a large, wet spot

63

forming on his light blue polo shirt from armpit to armpit, forming a perfect rectangle. He wasn't sweating, but suddenly realized that he had the sensation of warm water being slowly poured over his chest. He watched as waves seemed to leave his body and flow away from him across the room.

"It was weird. Not in a bad way, but just weird. I couldn't explain it. I felt at peace and energize at the same time! I looked over at my wife and said, 'I think the cancer just left my body'. Both my son and wife looked at me like I had lost my mind. My wife even came over and touched my face and neck to see if I was running a fever of something. I suddenly felt the need to move. I stepped down into the living room and just started prancing around like a little kid. I felt like my normal self. The exhaustion vanished."

Terri verifies his experience. "He had a wet patch going across his chest. I went over to feel his face and neck. I thought he was sweating, but he wasn't. He just had a large wet spot going across his shirt. Nowhere else, not his back or shoulders, just across his chest. I've never seen anything like it."

Later, they would realize that his was yet another miracle which they were experiencing for at that exact moment Dr. Nemeh was praying over his picture. This was a turning point from cancer and lymphoma to faith and inspiration for Steve and Terri.

"Looking back everything began to happen all at once," Terri says. "One moment I can't breathe, I'm being told my husband is going to be dead before our next anniversary. Before I can wrap my head around that we're being given hope. It seemed like every time I turned around it was another major thing happening. I was there and I am still amazed by what we went through. You don't have time to think. You just do what needs to be done."

As they were preparing to travel to Dr. Nemeh's office they decided to bring their granddaughter, Katelyn along. Katelyn had been experiencing rapid heart palpitations and had a couple fainting episodes while at school. She had been to see doctors in Ann Arbor, but they couldn't find anything wrong with her heart. She was placed on a heart monitor to determine the cause behind her episodes. Her family suspected that she might have Wolff-Parkinson White Syndrome.

Wolff-Parkinson White Syndrome is inherited through an affected parent. While neither Terri, nor Katelyn's father, Bryan had any symptoms to indicate they were afflicted, Terri's sister Liz did. Wolff-Parkinson White Syndrome is present at birth, though it is not something found during a routine physical. It is extremely rare, with less than 20,000 people per year being diagnosed. Symptoms such as dizziness, a rapid, pounding heartbeat, fatigue, anxiety, and fainting typically show up between ages of 11 to 50. Katelyn was thirteen. While anxiety and fatigue are common among most teenagers, fainting and a pounding heartbeat are not. At birth, persons who have inherited this syndrome have an extra electrical pathway located between the upper heart chamber or atria and the lower chambers, the ventricle. Electrical impulses which pump the blood from the heart are increased, causing the heart to beat faster. When this happens, the ventricles do not adequately fill with blood before it is pushing the blood into the body. This causes dizziness or fainting.

Whenever Katelyn's heart beat irregularly the monitor would beep. When this happened, she would have to write down exactly what she was doing at the moment. Since they would be leaving early to make their noon appointment with Dr. Nemeh, Katelyn spent the night with her grandparents. During the middle of the night, Terri remembers hearing the monitor making a sound she had never heard before. The beep was longer and somehow louder than usual. Katelyn must have thought the sound was different as well because she came racing out of the room so fast that she collided with the partially open door of the bedroom closet.

"Now of course we laugh when we remember how funny it was seeing Katelyn bounce off the walls like she was in a pinball machine. But then it was scary," Terri says of that night. Not only did she have her husband's condition to worry about, but she had her granddaughter's as well.

The next morning, Dana Beagle arrived to drive the Johnson family to Cleveland. Dana insisted on being with them, just like Steve was for Duncan all those years ago. Dana and her husband, Duncan had formed a close personal relationship with Dr. Nemeh and his wife Cathy over the years and though circumstances were less than ideal she was excited to introduce Steve and Terri to Dr. Nemehs.

That morning, Steve was really sick from the effects of the biopsy and most likely still weak from the shock of receiving a death sentence. His feelings of rejuvenation from the previous night were gone. He slept in the backseat the entire trip.

Photo of Steve and grandson Brody
received and prayed over by Dr. Nemeh.

Trust in the LORD with all your heart and lean not on your own understanding; in all your ways submit to him, and he will make your paths straight.

Proverbs 3:5-6

Once they arrived at Dr. Nemeh's office Dana, Katelyn, Terri, and Steve were escorted back to an examining room. After introductions, Dr. Nemeh requested that all other ailments be kept to themselves. He already knew that Steve had cancer. He wanted to pray over him. Terri watched as her husband was being prayed over and she began to feel a calm replacing her extreme anxiety. For an hour and a half, Dr. Nemeh prayed over Steve as he did an acupuncture treatment. After the acupuncture, the doctor continued to move his hands over Steve's body and continued to pray. His hands stopped over a rib Steve had broken years prior while wrestling with his sons. The rib had mended, but constantly ached.

"I was amazed. I took a deep breath and for the first time in decades the ache wasn't there. I hadn't even mentioned to the doctor that I had that pain. I had gotten in the habit of wearing a back brace because my back ached so much. For some reason when I left the house that day, I just chose not to wear it. I have no idea why I did that. When he stepped behind me, he told me that he could feel that I had a lot of back pain and said, 'Let me pray for that.' I felt him touching each vertebra and heard him tell my wife that he was separating the bones. As soon as he was done, he looked at me and smiled and told me, 'There you are now an inch taller.' We all laughed at that! He then told me that he got most of it. The back pain was gone. Any shred of doubt I had in the power of prayer was gone in that instant!"

A few days later, they would discover that an x-ray taken on his first visit to the oncologist revealed that the cancer had spread to the bones in his entire midsection, from his neck to the top of his thighs.

"I was astounded by the entire visit," Terri recalls. "Watching Dr. Nemeh praying over Steve, barely touching him was like nothing I'd ever seen before. Then he asked me about a hard bump in Steve's chest. I told him that Steve has had it for years. We couldn't remember when it appeared or even what it was from and it never seemed to hurt Steve. It was a round, marble sized hard bump. Dr. Nemeh prayed over it and told me to touch it again. I was surprised, it was flat. He prayed over it one more time and it was gone! He never even touched Steve!"

The pain in Steve's body was gone, he felt wonderful. Between his experiences a few days before with the waves leaving his body during Dr. Nemeh's prayers over his picture and how he felt at that minute he questioned whether he should begin the chemotherapy scheduled for the following week. Dr. Nemeh closed his eyes and started praying. After a few moments Dr. Nemeh's answer was, "yes". He was sure that Steve was receiving a healing, but he thought that Steve should continue with the treatment prescribed by the oncologist as well as to start taking a variety of supplements he recommended known to help prevent and fight cancer.

After he was finished with Steve, Dr. Nemeh turned to Katelyn. She had just watched as her Papa received a healing prayer and now it was her turn. Never laying his hands over her, he began to pray over Katelyn's heart. Terri watched as the doctor's hands turned from his normal color to a bright red.

"It looked like he had submerged them into scalding hot water," Terri says. "Never once did he touch her; it was like the stuff hurting her heart was coming out of her and into his hands." Her heart monitor has not gone off since this visit. Later, Katelyn's father Bryan would post on Facebook that Katelyn told him that it was as if "angels were tap dancing on my heart".

Leaving Dr. Nemeh's office Terri felt the doom and gloom she was plummeted into being replaced with hope. She now knew that she could be strong for Steve. She believed that she was given the strength to do whatever was needed of her, which as it turned out to be a lot. Looking back on that day, Steve says he wishes he had gone for another scan instead of beginning chemotherapy. However, he did as Dr. Nemeh advised and went through the treatment, and with the treatment came the side effects.

Cathy Nemeh, Steve Johnson, and Dr. Nemeh

*And the God of all grace, who called you to his
eternal glory in Christ, after you have suffered a
little while, will himself restore you and make
you strong, firm and steadfast*
I Peter 5:10

Chapter Six

Five, long, agonizing days after the biopsy, Steve, Terri and their youngest son, Bryan were once again sitting in a doctor's office waiting for the latest verdict. In this short period of time he already felt like he had been put through Hell. Looking over at his son and wife he wasn't sure how much more he could go through emotionally and worried about how much more they could endure. He wondered how many more doctor's offices they were going to visit before they heard some good news. How much time was this doctor going to tell him he had left? He was already feeling frustrated and discouraged. Before leaving his house that morning he again prayed asking God to give him something he could fight.

From the time of his initial diagnosis and sitting in the oncologist's office Steve continued to get weaker. He was rapidly losing weight, not eating and still tired. All he wanted to do was sleep.

Nearing tears, exhausted and dreading the thought of hearing another death sentence, the oncologist, Dr. Paul

Adams walked into the room. Steve looked the doctor straight in the eye and gave him the same request he had been asking of God. "Doc, give me something I can fight." This time, as the doctor shook his hand, he answered Steve with a smile and a look of hope in his eyes. "I think I may have just the thing."

Steve had been misdiagnosed; he did not have small cell lung cancer. He had Diffuse Large B Cell Lymphoma. A cancer with a very large percent of survival. This was one of the most common cancers. It is aggressive and is most common in men over sixty, Steve was 63. Some of the symptoms are the same as small cell lung cancer, unexplained weight loss, fatigue and loss of appetite. Had Steve not followed through with the biopsy and oncologist, he would have died during the time frame the pulmonologist had initially given him. The pulmonologist had made her diagnosis without the test results. She had informed the Johnson's that she had seen enough of these cases to be able to identify small cell lung cancer. The oncologist handed him something he could indeed fight with chemotherapy and God's amazing grace.

Dr. Adams felt that Steve should immediately start chemotherapy every three weeks for six treatments. The Lord had answered his prayers. He was given something that he could indeed fight. But he knew it wasn't something he was going to have to fight alone. He believed that fortified with God's grace he would be triumphant at the end of this battle.

This time the weakness he felt in his body and the difficulty in breathing were caused by the relief and joy that rushed over him. This was indeed game-changing news. He vowed that he was going to fight for his life and for his family. He was going to fight to be able to throw a ball with his grandson Brody. He was going to fight to be able to watch his granddaughter Katelyn go to her first dance. He had a life that still needed to be lived and he was going to fight for it.

Before he could begin chemotherapy, the next step was to have a port inserted into his chest. With the amount of treatments he would be receiving, having a port would eliminate having a needle put into his arm every time he went for a treatment.

The day he went into surgery he remembers praying. God willing, he believed he was going to kick this thing. He had been given something he could fight, and he was going to fight it like he's never fought before. His niece made a request on Facebook asking people to pray for her uncle. Almost immediately, people were responding with words of prayers, hopes for a complete healing and strength.

"I remember waking up from the anesthesia and seeing an angel floating above me. It was so quiet, I looked around to see if anyone else was there and if they could also see what I was seeing. I was overwhelmed with the sense peace. I immediately knew it was my guardian angel. I didn't feel scared or even shocked, I felt like I was floating too. She was supposed to be there. She wasn't there to escort me off this earth, that much I knew for sure! I believe she was sent to give me a message. I was going to win my fight and she was going to always be there. Now, years later, when I think about my guardian angel, I wonder if maybe she was sent by my mother to protect me."

With this new sense of peace from the Holy Spirit, he relaxed in preparation for battle.

Dr. Paul Adams and Steve Johnson

The Lord says, "I will rescue those who love me. I will protect those who trust in my name. [15] When they call on me, I will answer; I will be with them in trouble.
Psalms 91:14-15

If you abide in me, and my words abide in you, you shall ask what you will, and it shall be done to you.
John 15:7

Chapter Seven

Steve recalls the first time he walked into the Cancer Institute in Flint. Exiting the elevators on the second floor he walked into a large room lined with recliners. There was a 42" flat screen television hanging from the wall for anyone who was interested in the morning talk shows, and one portable television set which was being used by a patient. The walls were painted a nice but subdued color, and it was quiet, far too quiet for a room where at least a dozen or more people sat while the drugs prescribed to kill their form of cancer slowly dripped into their bodies. Each patient sat in a recliner. Patients had the choice of one of the recliners lined along the walls or one behind a curtained area which allowed for a little more privacy.

He signed in, selected a recliner and waited until the nurse arrived to insert a needle filled with his "designer" brand of chemo into the port in his chest. The entire nursing staff was very nice and efficient, but very busy. Steve watched as they moved about the room from patient to patient and for the first time ever, he was speechless.

"I couldn't think of one joke, one funny story, nothing. It was like I was struck mute! The nurses were very pleasant and tried to make everyone feel comfortable. I couldn't ask for better treatment, but I sure as Hell didn't want to be there!" Steve says.

Sitting there, looking around at the others, he almost felt guilty. Like him, they all had cancer of some kind and were in different stages of their treatment, but unlike them, he still looked healthy and walked in there without assistance. He realized that people avoided maintaining eye contact, briefly he wondered if they were feeling sorry for him because they knew what he was bound to experience next. Possibly, they were concentrating so hard on their own problems that they didn't even pay enough attention to him long enough to offer up more than a sympathetic thought or silent prayer. He still looked healthy, but for how long?

Another thing he didn't see in that room was hope. He didn't want to be there any more than the rest of them, in that they had common ground. He latched onto the knowledge that his prayers had been answered, *he* had something he could fight. He had Diffused Large B Cell

Lymphoma, not small cell lung cancer. Suddenly, a terrifying thought occurred to him: how many people in this room and around the world had a misdiagnosis? If not for the second opinion of Dr. Smith, he might possibly be one of the patients lying here without hope in his eyes, or worse sitting at home being destroyed from the inside by a cancer that was actually treatable. He knew he had to do something. He did what he does best...struck up a conversation with the person next to him. Maybe by sharing his story with someone they would feel hope and be helped. Looking around the room, he found his inspiration. A patient sitting nearby was wearing a Detroit Tigers Baseball T-Shirt.

Receiving chemotherapy was an all-day ordeal. Each time he went in, it took eight hours to receive the eleven different drugs prescribed for his cancer. He estimates that he spent about 48 hours total at the Cancer Institute. Anyone who knew Steve would say that they weren't surprised that he struck up conversations, he had the gift of gab, there was no way he could have been quiet for that long!

Steve began each treatment by greeting people as he walked by them, a simple good morning. Everyone responded in kind, but it was mechanically, no emotions. As cheerfully as he could, he struck up a conversation with the person seated next to him. Commenting on the Tigers baseball game, high school games, anything he could think of to liven up the place. Eventually, someone else would comment and before too long he had his small corner of the room laughing and forgetting their aliments for a few moments. Always conscious of others who were napping or at least trying to nap, he kept his level of noise to an intimate setting. When the nurses walked through to do routine checks on the patients, they became included in the jokes and stories.

Eventually, the chemotherapy would indeed take its toll on his body. He grew weaker and found it necessary to rely on a cane when walking. He never gave up his hope and continued to offer an encouraging word or prayers.

After Steve's first round of chemotherapy he felt fine. He was actually amazed at how great he felt. There were no signs of nausea and he even felt like he had a little energy. He had been told that chemo affects people in differently. He foolishly believed that he would be the one who wouldn't be as sick as others had been.

However, a few days later he realized the foolishness of his thought process. The vomiting hit with a vengeance. Even the smell of food sent him running for the toilet. Terri searched for something he could eat and keep down.

"I knew he had to keep his strength. It was a real ordeal feeding him. He would ask for things we didn't have in the house, things we rarely if ever ate. I'd drive to the store to buy the food he requested, get home, prepare it only to have him tell me that he wasn't hungry anymore or it didn't taste right."

Occasionally, he'd take a bite but throw it up within the hour. Then to add complications to the matter, his taste buds were changing. Things he used to love to eat he didn't like anymore, or he complained that they tasted like metal. Their son Bryan began researching foods which were healthy and brought them over hoping the nutrients would help combat the effects the chemo had on his father's body.

"After a while I discovered that he would eat the Frosty's from Wendy's. One time I went up there and the Frosty's were on sale for fifty cents. I bought five dollars worth to put in the freezer. This way Steve could eat it any time he wanted. He ate one and hasn't touched another one since!" Terri recalls with a laugh.

Steve started losing weight rapidly. Within three weeks, Steve was down 35 pounds. He had gone from 156 lbs. to 114 lbs. on his 5'8" frame. His hair started to fall out in clumps, so he shaved his head bald. As the weight melted off his body, he became increasingly cold. He joked that he felt part cat looking around for a sunny spot in the house to sit and warm his bones. He and his wife would sit out on their back deck in the early morning hours, before the sun's peak hours could cause any photosensitivity. Unless he was asleep, he was always 'too' something. Too cold, too tired, too ready to throw up.

Steve and his dog Bailey

Steve's days became routine. He would receive his chemotherapy, then less than a week later he was vomiting and feeling weak for the next two weeks. During these first two weeks, Terri would take him to the Cancer Institute several times to receive a bag of saline to keep him hydrated. He would receive visits by phone, take naps, lie on the couch and watch baseball. Then he would go to bed only to be woken up by another bout of vomiting. Morning would come with a repeat of the day before. He began to count down the days to that week before his chemotherapy when he felt normal again. During which time he felt well enough to eat a little so that he could regain his weight and strength for the next round of chemotherapy.

"The week before chemo was like being in training," Steve recalls as he shudders at the memory.

Other than the vomiting and weakness, the hardest part of this was not being able to see his grandson, Brody. Both he and Brody were used to being together several times a week while Brody's parents worked. Steve was told not to expose himself to any situations or environments where he may catch a cold or other virus. Unfortunately, that meant minimal contact with children. Steve tried talking with Brody on the phone, but the little boy's cries for Papa were enough to wrench out his heart. He promised Brody that as soon as he felt better and was not sick that they could play together. This was yet another promise Steve vowed to keep.

As active and social as Steve normally was, he started not wanting to leave his house. While the fear of exposure to viruses was real, he was more afraid of being too far from a bathroom. As his body was experiencing the side effects of chemotherapy, he never felt confident enough that he would not have an accident from one end or the other. Proudly he boasts, "I never made a mess, I always got to the bathroom in time!"

During Steve's illness his Facebook page was packed with people sending their well wishes and prayers. People neither he nor his wife knew were sending prayers and positive vibes towards his healing. Churches had him on their prayer lists and prayer chains. He had congregations as far away as Hawaii praying for him. Friends from high school, his refereeing family, and close personal friends and family were requesting information on how to help him during this time. Steve's 'Prayer Warriors' were on the job 24/7.

Family members mowed his lawn and asked for additional tasks to make his life easier. People graciously offered to sit with Steve so that Terri could go shopping or relax at the movies. Other than going to the store when she thought he might like to eat something; she maintained her vigil. As the offers and prayers poured in, she never left Steve's side.

Two months after Steve had received the healing powers of God, he felt well enough to post a message to Facebook thanking everyone for their prayers and support during this difficult time for he and his family.

"Emotions have turned me into my mother!" (June 23, 2016) Steve found himself crying at the amount of prayers and love being offered on a daily basis.

Everyone they knew offered their assistance in any manner needed. Throughout all the prayers, wishes of a speedy recovery, and love, his wife of 38 years was watching as her world was agonizingly unraveled, one day at a time.

As Terri watched Steve fighting for his life, she kept thinking that this wasn't how things were supposed to happen. This was the man with whom she had spent the last 40 years building a life and a future. She had his babies, was by his side when he decided to seek employment in Vegas, and now she was told it was coming to an end.

She had believed a month ago that they were at the stage of their lives where they were going to enjoy themselves. She retired from General Motors a few years earlier and was waiting for him to decide to retire as well. Their sons were adults with families of their own. They were enjoying their grandchildren. It was time for them to travel and do the things they always planned to do, but put off, while they were working to make the mortgage, changing diapers, and attending school events. All those dreams seemed to evaporate as Steve grew weaker and weaker.

Terri and Steve had so many friends and family who immediately reached out to them with offers of help. They were both grateful and moved by the amount of emotional support they were receiving, but there were times when Terri just wanted to hide away and cry as her heart was breaking. Then other times she just wanted to lie next to Steve and have him hold her in his arms for as long as they had left. She never allowed herself to think about him dying.

"I never really thought to plan his funeral," she explains. "I never let myself dwell on it, I couldn't, or I would have broken down. I kept my focus on one day at a time. I was too busy trying to get him to eat something and keeping him hydrated. This all seemed so unreal, like it wasn't happening to us."

Wavering between anger at this disease and feat that she was going to lose him, she was also frightened that she wasn't doing enough for him. Every moment away from him was a moment she could never get back. The more she tried to make him comfortable, the more irritated he became. He was not used to being sick and not being in control over what was happening in his body frustrated him. She knew his crossness wasn't directed at her; it was a side effect of the cancer. She was just the one who was there, like she promised all those years ago, "for better or worse, in sickness and in health". Sometimes she felt as if nothing she did was right. Terrified, she watched as he was literally wasting away before her eyes. His vomiting continued and he was growing weaker by the day.

One morning, as they were sitting on their back porch enjoying the sunshine and relaxing over a cup of coffee, Steve looked over to Terri and said, "You know you really are beautiful."

"My heart dropped into my stomach. Steve isn't one to come out and tell me I'm beautiful for no reason. I thought to myself, 'Oh my God, he believes he's going to die!' I didn't know what to do." Terri recalls.

On Father's Day, June 16, 2016, his son Bryan and daughter-in-law Sharlet posted a photo on Facebook of their children with Steve and Terri. At that time the prognosis was still grim, Steve had less than a year to live. This was going to be the photo Katelyn would be able to look at and remember her Papa, and the photo where Brody would be reminded of the man who had more plans than time to be his Papa.

Terri, Katelyn, Steve, and Brody Johnson

Bear your share of hardship along with me like a
good soldier of Christ Jesus.
2 Timothy 2:3

Chapter Eight

After a couple of treatment other complications set in. Steve became miserably constipated. During these phases he would receive scores of remedies from family and friends: eat prunes, use fiber drinks daily, eat apples. When the home remedies failed Steve and Terri decided to go old school and try an old fashioned, tried and true remedy, an enema.

Borrowing an enema bag from his sister, Sherry, he filled it with warm water and closing the bathroom door began his treatment. Terri offered her assistance, to which she was informed in no uncertain terms, "I got this." Squatting over the toilet he began the procedure, already relaxing at the thought of the relief he would soon receive.

"It was bad enough that I felt miserable and weak from my treatments, now I was uncomfortable and beginning to feel out of control! I'm the one who offers help, but learning to accept help, even from my wife was proving difficult. I was becoming a cranky old man. I needed relief."

Immediately the nozzle became clogged, frustrated Steve had to clean it out.

"It was disgusting! I was getting angry. At this point I thought I was going to have to dig it out one nozzle load at a time!"

A second time he began the procedure with the same results. Frustrated he decided that he did indeed need his wife's assistance. Calling to Terri from the bathroom he received stone silence. Tired, weak, irritable and in pain he called louder hoping to get her attention but received the same result. Realizing she must have gone outside to water the flowers he disengaged himself from the apparatus, went to the sink once again to clean the clogged nozzle. As he started rinsing the apparatus the pressure suddenly released and he could not get back to the toilet quick enough. Jumping into the tub, the instant relief in his body was so welcomed that he could only laugh at himself and the mess he stood in.
"Imagine a 62-year-old man standing naked in a mess that would make a two-year-old proud!"
Cleaning up after himself he took a much-needed shower and fell into a peaceful, pain-free slumber for the first time that week.
Steve experienced several bouts with constipation during his chemotherapy treatments.

"The severe pains usually hit in the middle of the night, between 2:00 and 4:00 am, always while I was sleeping."

Each time the pain hit Steve would sit on the edge of the bed trying to determine the best possibly position to alleviate the pain so he could go back to sleep. Terri would ask him if he wanted to go to the hospital. He always told her no, sometimes not very kindly.

"I didn't want to be that guy who called the ambulance every time he had a pain." His wife was concerned that his pride would be his downfall in the end. More often than not, he would go lay on the couch watching television to take his mind off his discomfort.

One night he recalls he woke up with pain so severe that he was actually worried that he was having a heart attack. He was sweating and gasping for breath as an agonizing pain in his chest spanned from shoulder to shoulder. He got out of bed and went to lie on the living room couch while his wife brought him a low dosage aspirin, just in case he really was having a heart attack.

"I was really scared, he had never been in that much pain before! After I gave him the aspirin, I ran to get the holy water Dana had given us. The words from the pulmonologist kept running through my head, 'he can't be revived'. Frantically, I started rubbing the holy water over his body and praying. I didn't stop until the pain went away. I've never been so scared in my life!" Terri shakes as she recalls the episode.

The next night began as a new nightmare of pain took hold. He had abdominal pain from the days of constant constipation, but this pain was worse than the night before. Getting out of bed he soon found himself doubled over on the bedroom floor groaning. Peering over the edge of the bed, feeling frustrated herself, Terri calmly asked, "Now are you ready to go to the hospital?" This time Steve agreed.

Arriving at Genesys Hospital in the middle of the night they were greeted to a packed waiting room. Terri immediately informed the nurse at the desk that Steve was a cancer patient. They were quickly whisked into a room to avoid unnecessary exposure to germs which could compromise his already weakened immune system. As soon as he was in the room a heart test was ordered to determine whether or not he was indeed having a heart attack. Quickly, that fear was laid to rest. Steve's heart was not the cause of his pain. With that worry laid to rest he was given morphine to make him comfortable while undergoing tests to determine the source of his pain.

Steve went through several different tests over the next few hours to locate the reason for Steve's pain. No sooner had the results from one test arrived when another test was ordered.

While Steve was in the hospital, he had many visitors... in between test. Many times, visitors would find Terri sitting alone in the hospital room waiting for the nurses to bring Steve back from the latest round of tests. Pat and Julie McKenna came to visit and were able to convince

Terri to go home for a few hours to get a much-needed rest. They assured her that they would stay until Steve returned from his tests and be there until she came back.

With so much of the focus being on the patient, the caregivers are most often overlooked during the long, horrific journey with any prolonged illness of a loved one. Caregivers may not experience the physical aspects of the illness, but the emotional toil is just as great, if not greater than those suffering. Watching someone you love dying is an agonizing drain on your mind and body. The helpless feelings compounded with the daunting task of taking care of someone you love while your heart is being ripped to shreds within your body is unimaginable. No one really knows what the individual is experiencing, and every case is as different as the disease itself.

"I never felt like leaving him alone. It's like having a newborn baby, you don't want to trust it to anyone but you," Terri explains. "Even a five-minute ride up to the store made me anxious. I didn't know what I would find when I returned."

As she left the hospital, she started looking forward to a long, leisurely shower and possibly a nap in her own bed before taking care of things which needed her attention.

"We had pets that needed feeding and a dog who needed to go outside. I had no idea what I would find when I got there!"

Steve's brother Butch and a few other friends also arrived to visit while Pat and Julie were there. Exhausted, and still medicated, Steve lay there trying to join in on their jokes and stories. When suddenly, without preamble, all of his visitors, except Julie and Pat McKenna were shuffled out as six different doctors filled his room. Each doctor offered up their expert opinion. Despite the six different recommended methods of treatment, they were all in agreement that he would need surgery to figure out the cause of his extreme discomfort. The chaos in the room was overwhelming. One minute he is visiting and laughing with family and friends and the next moment he is being bombarded with doctors wanting to cut him open. He began to feel panicky. He wanted his wife there by his side.

Terri did not hear her phone ring while she was in the shower. Physically, as well as emotionally exhausted she allowed the hot water to ease some of the tension from between her shoulders. Allowing her mind to go blank, she had just started to relax when she heard someone frantically banging on her front door. Quickly dressing to answer the door, she saw her neighbor. Immediately she could tell from the expression on his face that something was very wrong. In that instant the tranquil moment she had experienced vanished and the tension returned to her shoulders.

The neighbor explained that Steve had called from the hospital in an agitated state. Steve had tried to call her and when she didn't answer he called the neighbor; he needed her back at the hospital with him immediately. Without hesitation she got ready to return to the hospital.

Steve didn't want surgery, but he was willing to do whatever it took to get rid of the pain.

"All these doctors were there talking about operating, they weren't even talking to me! It was chaos! I couldn't even think before another doctor would start talking about a different operation. When all of a sudden Dr. Faris walked into the room. It was like a ray of sunshine breaking through dark storm clouds. I felt like I was covered in warmth, it was a message to put my trust into this man! I stopped even listening to those other guys, Dr. Faris was the one I could hear!"

Pat and Julie McKenna were still with Steve when Dr. Faris explained his method of getting to the cause of the problem. Turning his focus to Steve and Pat's wife, Julie, he began by saying,

"You're going to love me and hate me for what I'm about to do to you."

Dr. Faris continued by telling them that he wanted to order one more test before he would even entertain the idea of surgery. He explained that he wanted to order a CT scan to see exactly what was going on inside of Steve's body. The part Steve was going to hate was the procedure in which he was going to receive the liquid prior to the scan. Fearing that Steve would puke up the liquid, the doctor wanted to administer it through a tube which would be inserted through his nose.

Putting his trust in the doctor and, also wanting to avoid surgery, he didn't hesitate as he nodded his head in agreement. While waiting for the liquid to arrive, the doctor and Steve fell into an easy conversation. He told Steve that he thought he recognized him but wasn't sure from where. Having heard this statement countless times before, Steve asked if he followed high school sports at all. Instantly, Dr. Faris knew why he recognized his newest patient. Steve had officiated several of his son's ball games.

The nurse arrived with the prescribed liquid and quickly inserted the tube into Steve's nose. Three 32-ounce bags of something that looked like liquid chalk was quickly pumped into his body. Time was of the essence; he needed to get the scan before his body forced him to expel the liquid, causing them to start the unpleasant procedure all over again. While Steve was lying in his hospital bed getting liquid pumped through his nose, his friend John Montney's mother Beth was standing outside his door praying for him.

Lying still and focusing on relaxing, he was quickly wheeled down the hall to be scanned. Two young nurses in training were given the task of taking him for the scan. He remembers how they chatted to each other, laughing and having no empathy for his need to relax. Steve felt that they were acting as if they were wheeling down a food tray, not a patient.

Fearing repercussions from any suggestions of them to be quiet, he laid there silently while his frustration grew. He wanted to get there quickly, get the scan and have them gone.

"I knew I was angry and that my best bet was to keep my mouth shut. I didn't want to be bounced off the wall or their pace to slow but damn, everything about them irritated me."

As soon as the scan was taken and he was safely back in his room, the process of extracting the liquid began. It had to be taken out the same way it went in...through a tube in his nose. One full jar was extracted when the tube clogged. His rising irritability was soon overridden by the need to vomit. Grabbing the little green puke bag by his bedside he proceeded to expel the remaining two jars worth.

"Whoever designed that little green puke bag is a genius!" Steve exclaims. "That bag is a lifesaver. I never made a mess," He proudly states.

By the time the test results were in, Terri had made it back to the hospital. When Dr. Faris walked into the room he was greeted by Steve and another woman, his wife Terri. Before he began explaining the results he politely asked, "Who are you?"

"I must have looked at him like he had three heads when I pointed at Steve and said I was his wife," Terri laughs.

Not realizing that when he first met Steve that the woman in the room wasn't his wife he had responded to her questions as if she was. He had no way of knowing that Julie was not Steve's wife. Laughing over the error, Dr. Faris announced that surgery was definitely not necessary. Steve's pain was caused from being constipated. The doctor went on to explain that the liquid used for the CT scan might help loosen his bowels. They would wait until morning to see how things were before they made any other decisions. Relieved to have a diagnosis not requiring surgery and his wife by his side, he began to relax and get some much-needed rest.

Around 4:00 a.m., true to form, Steve was woken up. Looking over to his wife he told her that he felt like he needed to use the bathroom. Wheeling his I.V. stand into the bathroom he saw a little, white, plastic bowl inserted under the toilet seat to gather a stool sample when he was ready. Quickly filling the bowl he looked up to see the night nurse standing there, "Come on in!" he called, "We're having a shitty party!" Laughing at himself he then apologized to the woman for the mess he was making. Smiling down at him she stated, "Honey, don't you worry about me. I'm just happy for you!"

After filling tree bowls, the nurse began helping him get cleaned up and back to bed. Looking over at the third sample bowl, now overfilled, he laughed as he asked his nurse, "Do you think that will be enough for a stool sample? I think I lost another 36 pounds right there!"

As soon as he got into bed he realized that for the first time in several days he was hungry. He asked the nurse how soon will breakfast would be served.

"Once the food arrived and I began to eat I was so amazed at how much a simple act could bring me such joy. Everything tasted wonderful! I was so happy."

Later that day Steve was talking to the day nurse as she was taking his vital signs. She told him that she had never seen so many doctors in one room in all of the the years she had worked at this hospital. Looking at her Steve replied, "Well I sure as Hell didn't invite them!"

Laughing with him, Steve quickly realized that he had been given an opening. Straight faced he continued by telling her that they were requesting all kinds of things from him. Unwittingly, she took the bait and asked what kinds of things were they asking. He responded by saying,

"They wanted a bunch of things. One wanted a stool sample, another one wanted a urine sample, and a sperm sample. I told them to check my underwear."

Seeing the twinkle in his eyes as he tried to suppress his grin she started laughing. Still laughing, the nurse asked Steve to roll onto his side so that she could check for bed sores. Steve told her she could check but only on one condition. Cautiously she asked him what was the condition. He explained to her that he had lost so much weight during his illness, places that were once toned with muscles had been reduced to saggy wrinkled skin. Nodding her head as she listened, sympathy in he eyes, he told her, "You can only check if you promise not to laugh at my sharpei ass."

   Laughing with him, the nurse told him that she would do her best as he rolled over. Stories of his jokes soon spread like wildfire through the entire hospital floor.

 "I wish I knew the names of the floor nurses who took care of me while I was there. They were all very professional as well as being personable. They were wonderful," Steve tells people of his stay in the hospital. "They couldn't have been nicer to me and my wife if I had been their own family."

   Steve would end up spending nine days in the hospital. Quickly, he became a favorite patient amoung the nurses. No matter how tired or sick he was, he always had a joke for them.

Pat and Julie McKenna

Beth Montney

There are different kinds of gifts, but the same
Spirit distributes them. ⁵There are different
kinds of service, but the same LORD.
⁹to another faith by the same Spirit, to another
gifts of healing by that one Spirit
Corinthians 12:4-5,9

Chapter Nine

The next time Steve spoke with Dr. Nemeh, it was through FaceTime. Steve had started his chemotherapy and as is typical with chemo, wasn't responding well. He felt fine for four or five days, then by the end of the week the side effects hit him hard. He was sick, constantly vomiting and then sleeping. He was so weak that he did not even have the strength to sit up and hold the phone. Talking was an effort as well.

Terri held the phone to his ear so that Steve could hear Dr. Nemeh. As he lay there listening to Dr. Nemeh's words, he felt an inner peace. Physically he felt awful, but somehow, he also felt something else...that flicker of hope. At that moment Dr. Nemeh told Steve that he needed to connect more with and surrender to God. It had to be more than just saying that he believed, Steve was told that he had to have faith with his whole heart. He had to trust God to take over and do **His** work. Steve's priorities had to change.

Jesus replied, "What is impossible with man is possible with God."
Luke 18:27

In 1969 Swiss psychiatrists, Elizabeth Kubler-Ross and David Kessler presented the five stages of grief people experience when faced with a traumatic event; denial, anger, bargaining, depression, and acceptance. Later, she added two additional stages with shock being the first stage and testing coming before acceptance.

The shock, or first stage of grief was the immediate response Steve and Terri experienced when they received Steve's death sentence. Both Steve and Terri have often said that they felt like this was being told to someone else, not them. They couldn't seem to process the words, "Do you have a will?" and "You have two or three months to live." They heard the words and understood the meaning but could not understand how something like this could happen to them. Terri has said on many occasions,

"We are good people. We don't cheat on our taxes, we follow the rules, how can this be happening to us?"

The remaining stages of grief, denial and anger came together, and they came quick. One moment they were, "mad as Hell," according to Steve. Then the next moment he would think that he couldn't have lung cancer. He never smoked. While he wasn't a 'health nut', he didn't abuse his body either. He was active, physically fit and

101

other than suddenly being a 62- year- old man who felt like he needed a nap, he was fine.

During the first three stages, while he was still angry, he decided he wasn't going to spend the last remaining six months sick from chemo and/or radiation. He was just going to enjoy the time he had left loving his family and trying to build happy, lasting memories. He was most angry and incredibly sad at the thoughts of missing his grandchildren growing up. That realization made his heart ache with a pain he had never known before.

"I cried when my mom died, thinking of missing Katelyn and Brody's childhood really brought on the waterworks."

Some people have a 'come to Jesus' moment while others are willing to try any avenue available, spending large amounts of money to find a cure. Steve realized that he had a lot to fight for and forfeiting was not in his nature. He asked God to give him something to fight and fight was what he planned to do. Steve was ready to bargain.

Cannabis, in the form of medical marijuana is gaining popularity for the treatment of cancer in the United States. If you ask 100 physicians about a cure for cancer, you'll get 100 different answers. There are as many opinions as there are types of cancer. One however, which seems to be growing in popularity is 'pot pills', Canabidiol (CBD) oil in a capsule. In the first few days of his diagnosis, Steve was approached by a friend to try this avenue.

In the United States, the Food and Drug Administration (FDA) has not approved the use of marijuana, making it an illegal substance. Marijuana is classified as a Schedule I substance in the United States because it is considered potentially addictive. Some states, such as Colorado, Alaska, and Michigan have passed laws which allow both recreational and medicinal dispensaries to legally operate.

The National Cancer Institute has not endorsed medical marijuana as a 'cancer curing' drug but has endorsed its usage to treat the symptoms associated with chemotherapy and radiation. Nausea and loss of appetite are two of the most common complaints for cancer patients. It is also being used more widely to help patients sleep soundly, allowing their bodies to rest and recharge. Medical marijuana, however, is not recommended for children because there is a fear that it can affect brain development.

Steve went on the Internet and began researching medical cannabis. He read a blog where a woman had terminal cancer and without her doctor's knowledge used cannabis along with the chemo treatment. Within months, this woman's tumor had drastically shrunk. As he continued his research, he read other success stories linked to cannabis with and without chemo and radiation. Steve began to think that perhaps he would try the cannabis alone. What was the worst thing that could happen to him? He was dying, getting addicted did not seem like something to be concerned about and it certainly was not going to kill him. Recalling this experience, he says,

"Looking back, it seems like so many things started falling into place for me. My first batch of CBD oil capsules came from Oregon. I didn't order them, I didn't even ask for them, they came from a friend."

He knew someone who just lost an acquaintance to cancer. This man and his wife had decided to try the pills, but they arrived shortly after the man had died. They were offered to Steve. 200 capsules were received. Like the woman from the blog, he decided that he wasn't going to tell his doctor. Steve and Terri both knew that he needed to eat in order to maintain his strength and try to gain weight. They hoped that this would at least help with that aspect. The prescribed dosage was one pill a day.

When asked if she felt the pills helped her husband, Terri shrugs her shoulders and replies that,

"Steve seemed to relax, and he was definitely more interested in eating during the days prior to receiving the next round of chemo. He wasn't what we would have called 'stoned' back in high school. He was able to sit still and gain back some of the weight he had lost during the week he was so sick after treatment."

Asking Steve if he believes the CBD pill helped him, he just smiles and responds with, "I don't remember."

While Steve and Terri definitely flirted with the depression stage of grief, they were always too busy fighting to allow it to take hold. Terri has repeatedly said that she couldn't allow herself to dwell on the, 'whys and what ifs'. They simply didn't have time to get depressed. They never gave up. Acceptance wasn't an option either. "I wasn't going down without a fight." Steve says.

Steve will never forget sitting in Dr. Adams office after he had received his last chemotherapy treatment. Feeling good he was ready to what ever the doctor prescribed. Dr. Adams walked into the examination room, shook Steve's hand and announced, "Your cancer is gone."

"When he told me that, I was scared to believe it was really over. I kept a hold of his hand and said, 'don't mess with me, man.' I thought I was going to cry when he told me that he doesn't joke about things like this and that I was in complete remission! I didn't know what to do! I grabbed him and gave him a big hug. I don't think I've stopped smiling since!"

Shortly thereafter, Steve began to notice changes in his body. One morning, as he got out of bed, he noticed an unusual amount of dry skin on the bedsheets. He had always had extremely dry skin, but never had so much flaked off his body in the middle of the night. There was a layer of dead skin coating the insides of his pajamas as well.

"It was really weird! I got out of the bathtub and saw a layer of dead skin floating on top of the water like an oil slick. It wasn't just in chunks, but one large piece that covered the entire tub. It looked like I had shed me old skin, like a snake. Since then my skin has not been as dry as it has been my entire life. It has only happened to me that one time."

He also started enjoying foods that he refused to eat before, especially pancakes. "I have no idea why I didn't like them, but now I order them every chance I get!"

Steve's cancer has been in complete remission for a little more than two years at this point. A miracle he credits, "by the hand and mercy of God!"

As an official for many of the high school sports, he was well known with the coaches, the players and many of the fans. People who have never personally met Steve have followed his story on the local news. Between the local news station and newspapers covering his story, people often recognize him wherever he goes.

"I was at the new buffet restaurant walking back to my seat with a full plate of food and a lady stopped me. She said, 'hey aren't you that guy on t.v.?' I stood and talked to her for several moments. I showed her my picture. Then listened as she and her husband spoke of a loved one who has cancer. Right there in the middle of the restaurant I said, 'let's pray for their healing' It happens all the time. It doesn't bother me. I can't share enough the miracle given to me through God's unconditional love."

People will reach out to him and ask for a hug or to pray for them or a loved one. Steve never declines an offer to share a prayer or offer a kind and hopeful word. When he tells someone that he understands their misery and pain, he is speaking from the heart and his own experience.

He was soon being asked to share his inspirational story at churches and sporting banquets. The local news station did a follow up piece on him and was there to welcome him back to his first high school basketball game, Carman Ainsworth versus Grand Blanc.

The very first speaking engagement he accepted was at a local church. Steve has many experiences speaking in front of people. He has been the auctioneer for many fundraising events, the master of ceremonies several times and of course has been interviewed countless times but speaking in front of a church congregation was a new experience for him.

Steve has never written the speech he wants to deliver, he thinks about what he wants to say, jots down a note or two, but never writes it down. This speaking engagement would be no different. He did what came natural to him, he started with a joke. He introduced himself and immediately went on to tell his audience that he had been worried that he was going to be late today because of an incident at the gas station.

"I was standing there, pumping my gas, minding my own business, when I saw a woman's arm burst into flames. She started waving it around, like she was trying to put out the flames, but that only made it worse. I didn't have time to think about anything except helping that poor woman. Before I could get to her a police officer tackled her to the ground, extinguished the fire and proceeded to handcuff the poor woman!"

Pausing for dramatic effect, a collective gasp went through the congregation at this poor woman's ordeal.

"I was shocked! I couldn't believe what I was seeing! I yelled, 'Officer, what are you doing? I saw the entire thing, she didn't do anything wrong. Why are you arresting her?' The officer looked right at me and said, 'I'm arresting her for waving a *fire arm* in public."

The audience laughed. The ice was broken. Not only has he been asked back many times, but one of the church ladies told him that she enjoyed listening to him so much that the next time he comes back she is going to make him a pecan pie.

Steve always explains that even in the midst of this horrible illness, he always felt blessed. He wasn't an overly religious man through his adulthood, attending church only when he had to for a wedding or funeral. As a kid he was required to go to church with his parents. He would tell people that he owned a Bible and could probably tell you where it was located, but he never really opened it until he became the recipient of one of God's miracles.

"I have decided that as many times as I've been asked to join a church that I'm going to have to say no. I don't want to be tied to just one church, just one faith. I want to share my miracle with everyone regardless of church affiliation or religious belief. I believe God has called me to minister to all by sharing my story with as many people as I can."

Steve gets daily requests to visit and pray for sick loved ones who are at hospitals or their homes. His Facebook page continues to be flooded with prayer requests and Steve does his best to accommodate everyone he gets. At a recent fund-raiser for a young girl fighting cancer he was able to have a conversation with Coach Tom Izzo. "I've met him a few times while officiating, but this time we weren't working." Steve says with a smile of someone he admires and respects a great deal. Steve also continues to support Flint youth baseball.

MSU Coach Tom Izzo and Steve Johnson

Tom Cole Classic Fund Raiser
Judge Duncan M. Beagle, Steve Johnson, John Montney, and
Judge Thomas C. Yeotis

Since his remission, Steve and Terri have been blessed with another grandson, Teddy. True to his word he has started slowing down a bit; he and Terri have started traveling a bit and enjoying their (semi-) retirement years. They have been back to Las Vegas twice to visit friends and enjoy being a tourist in a place they once called home. He also was able to be at his wife's side when she lost her sister Liz at the age of 79. He's making plans again, plans with his wife to watch their grandchildren grow. He plans to see his granddaughter Katelyn graduate and his son Bryan walk her down the aisle at her wedding. He has plans to play ball with his grandsons, Brody and Teddy. His grandchildren will grow up knowing their Papa in person, not through photos and stories told by friends and family.

Steve has returned to officiating high school basketball and football. He is a bit sad at not being able to officiate baseball any longer, due to the prolonged exposure to the sun. He misses it but counts his blessings to have been as involved with the game for so many years and on many different levels. He has many fond memories associated with the game, both as a player and an official. He still watches the game and follows the Detroit Tigers. He also has two grandsons with which he intends to pass on the knowledge, love, and respect of the game.

During Thanksgiving weekend 2018, he officiated the Michigan High School Athletic Association (MHSAA) Division 1 football tournament finals at Ford Field in Detroit, Clarkston vs. Chippewa Valley (31-30 final score). Fox Sports Detroit News was there to cover the game and his story. During the fourth quarter of the game the sportscaster began discussing his story for the viewing audience. While showing the photo of him at his worst stage of cancer, they marveled at his recovery. Not only had he recovered but he was able to return to something he loves, at the highest level of the high school football division, the MHSAA.

Steve Johnson on the big screen during the MSHAA division finals
(reprinted with permission by the MSHAA)

Steve asked God to give him something he could fight. God answered his prayers. Steve got his life back.

The Johnson Family
Steve, Teddy, Terri, Katelyn and Brody

Brad and Steve Johnson

Aaron Johnson (nephew), Bryan Johnson (son), Brad Tippett (nephew), and Steve Johnson

*Give thanks to the LORD, for he is good. His love
endures forever.*
Psalm 136:1

Chapter Ten

The first time I actually met Dr. Nemeh was a year and a half after Steve had been cancer-free. We had already decided to write the book when Steve and Terri invited me to witness for myself Dr. Nemeh in action. I had already started reading the book, "Miracles Everyday" by Maura Postom Zagrans, written about people's interactions with the Holy Spirit through Dr. Nemeh's intervention and was intrigued.

Excitedly I grabbed my notebook and pen and headed out for a 45-minute drive from my home. I wasn't sure what to expect. I just knew that Steve, along with thousands of others had put their trust in Dr. Nemeh's hands. I also saw an opportunity to interview Judge Beagle and his wife, Dana.

Spiritual or Faith Healing can stir up negative images of T.V. evangelists from the early 1970's. I purposely didn't tell anyone where I was going because I didn't want their negativity clouding my experience. I was not looking to debunk Dr. Nemeh's abilities, nor was I planning on bringing anything less than a positive, open mind.

When Steve said he was going to ask Dr. Nemeh to pray over me I politely told him, "No, but thanks." People were coming to see Dr. Nemeh with serious, life threatening ailments. My complaints were trivial, I had high blood pressure and an underactive thyroid. I wasn't going to ask for a healing when others, who had traveled far and wide were hoping for a miracle to cure them of cancer or another serious ailment.

I expected to walk into an auditorium filled with people, with a stage set up front and multi-colored lights shining on the stage. What I found was quite the exact opposite. A small conference room was set up in a hotel with approximate seating for 150 people. There was no stage, no lights, just a podium and a microphone. Surprisingly, the space felt intimate and welcoming.

As we entered the lobby of the hotel, Dr. Nemeh was pointed out to me. My first impression of Dr. Nemeh was that he was not seeking the limelight, he didn't feel himself to be a superstar, and as the day proceeded that demeanor continued. I was immediately surprised to see that he wasn't surrounded by a mob, nor was he trying to be elusive. If I had been there on my own as a first-time visitor, I would not have noticed him at all. He was milling around the lobby with the rest of the people, stopping to greet someone here and there. People weren't trying to get to him to tell him of their illness before the presentation began, Dr. Nemeh was simply trying to make everyone who came feel welcome.

Steve pulled me over to Dr. Nemeh and introduced us. Behind thick glasses, his eyes warmed and seemed to pull me into his inner circle as if I were the most important person in all of the world to him. A reflection on how God feels for each of us. With great enthusiasm, Steve looked at me and said, "This man is amazing! Thank you, Dr. Nemeh!" The doctor just shook his head and in his gentle, accented voice said, "It is not me. Thank Jesus. It is all *Him*. I just prayed for you."

During the few moments we visited in the lobby with dozens of people milling around, I never felt he was trying to hurry me along so that he could meet with the next person. Steve introduced me as, "the author" of the book about his journey. Dr. Nemeh was completely engage in our conversation, asking questions about my progress, wishing me success, and expressing an interest to read it soon. As his wife Cathy joined us to retrieve him to start the presentation, he put his hand on my shoulder, smiled and said, "We'll talk again." I felt like he was truly interested in hearing what I was saying and not just being polite.

His wife of more than 30 years began the afternoon with an introduction of her husband. Siting in the front row, with my pen posed above my notebook, I listened as she talked about her husband's dedication with his patients at his medical practice just outside of Cleveland. She spoke of many nights where she waited quite late in the evening for him to return home. He would explain to her that his last patient needed to be reassured and very often, to pray with them. A devout Catholic, Dr. Issam Nemeh has always been happy to share the Holy Spirit with others.

Cathy Nemeh then went on to share a story with the audience about a conversation she and her husband had one evening while eating a late dinner. Sharing his belief in the power of prayer, she asked him how he saw himself in God's mission. He quietly left the room and returned with a picture of Jesus surrounded by a crowd of people as he rode into town on a donkey. Dr. Nemeh said to his wife that he sees himself as the one closest to Jesus in the picture. Studying the framed picture he had removed from a wall in their home, she pointed out a couple of the people who were reaching out to Jesus or standing close to him. With each guess he would smile and gently shake his head, no. He pointed to the donkey on which Jesus was riding, the one carrying Jesus on his back to bring him to the people who needed him. He tells his wife that he is the one, the donkey who brings Jesus to the people. He does not heal people, Jesus does.

As soon as Dr. Nemeh walked into the room I could feel the energy around me change. The excitement from the people in the room was so great that it became contagious. There was a physical presence, there was hope.

Dr. Nemeh began by expressing to the audience the love God has for each and every one of us. How *He* wants us to ask for Him, not for Him to force His way into our hearts. As Dr. Nemeh spoke, I felt like he was talking specifically to me, looking directly at me, not a room full of people. His voice gently reminded me that God had a special purpose for me, that all *He* asks is that I open my heart, forgive my enemies, and accept the gifts *He* gives me every day. Dr. Nemeh talked for what seemed like a minute or two, gently, gracefully, but given the message he delivered it was more likely to have been an hour. He never once spoke of himself, nor of the many success stories associated with his delivery of God's message, just that God was ready for me and I needed to be ready to receive Him. Occasionally I would hear someone behind me say, "Amen" or murmur an agreement which startled me, as I had forgotten that others were also in the room with me.

The podium was eventually removed, and people were then invited to come up to pray with Dr. Nemeh. Children were invited first, but everyone who wanted a healing prayer would receive one. He would be there as long as people wanted his prayers for their healing.

People began to come forward with children to be prayed over. An additional row of 10 to 12 chairs were placed in the very front of the room. Closely I watched as the doctor prayed over them. I had read that a man who had a brain tumor believed that he saw a black spot fall to the floor between he and Dr. Nemeh as he was receiving a healing prayer. Steve himself has stated repeatedly that when his photo was being prayed over that he saw waves leaving his body at the site of his cancer. I don't know if I expected to see sparks flying from other people's heads, but I do know that I could see their shoulders relax and their posture improve, as if the heavy weight of their illness was being lifted from their shoulders.

I witnessed one young girl around 13 years old, who required a walker to get around come to the front of the room. Her fingers were tightly bent on the armrest even when she wasn't moving. When the doctor came to her and began praying and touching her spine, I saw her fingers start to relax and her hands unclenched; her heart was open. I did not witness pyrotechnics, or black spots, I witnessed the true belief and complete trust of people in God, people who were ready for *His* healing presence.

> *"Take heart..." He said, "Your faith has healed you..."*
> *Matthew 9:22*

With each prayer, the room remained quiet and respectful of others who were praying or being prayed over. There were not any loud outbursts or sobbing, no one screaming for God's mercy, just calm, heartfelt praying for themselves and others. I looked up and realized that Dana Beagle was motioning for me to come up for a healing. I shook my head, but she gave me a look that said she would not take no for an answer. Her husband was already in the front row waiting for his healing prayers, turned and looked at me. Smiling he told

121

me, "My wife says get up here, you get up here."
Reluctantly, I put my paper and pen on my chair and took
the empty seat next to Duncan.

As I sat there waiting, I worried. I had nothing worthy of
a healing prayer. I was relatively healthy. My complaints
were trivial. People had driven from other states, who
were dying of a disease or were confined to a wheelchair,
like Duncan Beagle, they were asking for prayers. I felt like
a fraud sitting there, unworthy of a prayer that others
needed so much more.

Since I was up there and healthy, I decided that I'd
better make sure that I could receive a healing prayer and
not waste anyone's time. I did what the doctor suggested
we all do. I let go of my negativity. I forgave my enemies,
I let go of my petty jealousy to open a path for God's
healing grace.

Duncan Beagle and I were seated in the middle of the
row. Focusing on spiritually preparing myself I lost touch
with time. I am not sure how many minutes I sat there,
praying, asking for forgiveness when I sensed Dr. Nemeh
approach Duncan and his wife Dana. While I could not
hear the words he said, I could hear the warm gentle
sound of his voice. I did not need to hear his words; I
heard His love. A relaxing sense of protection came over
me and I realized that I was praying for the judge as well. I
watched as Dana looked at her husband with hope and
love, love for more than just her husband, love for the
miracle she knew Jesus was going to give them when the
time was right. I felt a cooling breeze coming off of the

judge on to my right knee and thigh. It was a refreshing breeze like one after a spring rain, not cold or numbing, just gentle and fresh. Dana looked at me with a smile that radiated from her soul through to her eyes and asked, "Do you feel that warm breeze?" Suddenly the rest of the room seemed to have melted away, it was the three of us sharing this intimate moment of faith for Duncan's healing. I told her it felt cool on my side. Smiling, she turned to her husband and asked, "Are you ready to stand?" Dana felt warmth, I felt cool, Duncan felt tingling in his legs. I believe that each of us received our own individual message from God. I saw Duncan's foot twitch. Dr. Nemeh placed a hand on Duncan's shoulder, smiled into his eyes, and whispered, "Soon." Neither Duncan nor Dana expressed disappointment at not receiving an instant miracle. They have faith. When the time is right, Duncan Beagle will walk again.

Still nervous, I stood with Dr. Nemeh. When he asked me what bothered me, I told him that I have high blood pressure. Looking at me, that caring smile reaching his eyes, he shook his head and very softly said, "No, you have headaches." Without thinking I nodded. He then told me he was going to pray for my headaches and for the stressors which caused those headaches. As an elementary teacher in an urban setting, my mind was flooded with images of the things which caused stress. Placing his hands on my shoulders he began to pray. Closing my eyes, again I felt like the entire room had disappeared and it was just the doctor and me. I heard his voice and occasionally I heard words, but I also heard a steady, pleasant humming sound, not the buzzing sound I get when my blood pressure is rising. I was calm inside, I no longer worried that I didn't have the right to ask for his prayers.

As Dr. Nemeh continued to pray for me, I felt his fingers travel along my spine, stopping and gently pressing a spot here and one there before continuing down my back. He stopped momentarily around the middle of my back and I distinctly felt three fingers applying pressure. It was like the grip used to hold a bowling ball. I heard him praying for my family and then it felt like he was turning a knob in my back. The grip, the pressure, the movement, I expected to feel a jolt of pain, or hear a popping sound of my spine being adjusted but none of that happened. I don't remember sitting down, I just know that I was relaxed and content to just be there. I wasn't thinking about anything. I'm not sure how long I sat there when I heard Duncan talking to me. He was smiling at me as he spoke, but all I heard was a pleasant humming sound as if I was being reassured by angels that all would be fine in my world.

Since I lost my brother from cancer, I have a desire to let as many people as possible know that miracles do indeed still happen because God is still performing them. I witnessed a miracle in Steve Johnson. Miracles happen every day, even if we do not recognize them.

"...for today is holy to our Lord. Do not be saddened this day, for rejoicing in the Lord must be your strength!"
Nehemiah 8:10

Author's Note

People have asked why I decided to write about Steve's journey. How am I involved? The answer is simple. His story needs to be told if for nothing other than to give hope to others. My youngest brother died from cancer. I wish I had known about Dr. Nemeh and The Prayer Warriors 7 months earlier.

When Steve was diagnosed, I had known him for about three years. I met Steve through his brother and sister-in-law, Nancy. Nancy had been my neighbor for 10 years. Four of those years were after she had married Steve's brother Butch. My husband and I bowled on a league with Butch and Nancy for many years. One of those years Steve and Terri bowled on the league as well. I remember during that year laughing at his jokes and watching him go from team to team visiting everyone, telling jokes and teasing people about their bowling. No one was immune, everyone was included when Steve was around. Every week he had new jokes and funny stories to tell. Even if he had already told it weeks earlier, his delivery made it hilarious all over again. Sometimes just hearing him laugh at his own joke was infectious enough to have others laughing with him. His teammates only had to locate the source of laughter to find Steve when it was his turn to bowl. His energy was infinite. It was amusing watching him bowl then go off and visit other teams. He was a one-man cheer squad on that bowling league.

Still, that encounter with him probably wouldn't have been enough of a reason for me to want to tell his story. I would say I watched Steve's story unfold from the sidelines, but when you meet Steve you're never on the sidelines. He includes you. He has an ability to make a person feel like they are the most important person to him and one of his nearest and dearest friends.

I found out about Steve's cancer the same way everyone else did, through Social Media. His brother, Butch posted on Facebook that he needed everyone to pray for his brother. People who know Butch know that he isn't one to ask for something unless he feels there are no other alternatives, and prayers aren't something he ever mentions. So, when that post came across people, including me, called to ask him what was wrong that Steve needed our prayers. Was he injured in a car accident? Sadly, my first thought, knowing that Steve was extremely active and in his early 60's was... 'Oh no! Steve has had a heart attack.' My thoughts probably would have been much more preferable than the battle with cancer he was about to embark upon.

Almost immediately, Steve, Terri, Butch, and Nancy were bombarded with texts and phone calls. "What is wrong with Steve?' I doubt anyone thought about cancer.

He was too healthy. He was too active. But then again, people don't usually look at someone and think, 'He'd better stop what he's doing, or he'll get cancer', unless of course they are heavy smokers.

Soon I, along with hundreds of others became the team Steve called his personal "Prayer Warriors" and thanks to Facebook, Butch and Nancy, we were able to spiritually follow and support him on this dark path through his journey.

The main reason I wanted to get his story out there is to help people like me and my family. Seven months earlier, I lost my youngest brother Rob to cancer. Watching the miracle happen with Dr. Nemeh, I ran through thousands of emotions. We, like so many other families of cancer sufferers, didn't know where or who to turn to when Rob got worse. We felt helpless. The doctors would give us a look which did not give us hope and shake their heads. When our mother, devastated as she watched her youngest child get sicker by the day, asked if there was anything more we could do, anything else we could try. Always, she heard the same answer, "Go home and make him as comfortable as possible for the time he has left."

Often, people tend to take a doctor's word as gospel. When they say there is nothing else to do, we tend to take that as a message that the end is near. We did what we were told. We took Rob home and tried to make him comfortable. We helped him get his affairs in order and contacted family members so that they had an opportunity to say goodbye.

Rob was only 48 when he passed away. I wish we had heard of Dr. Nemeh seven months earlier. He was 3 years and 9 months younger than me and 2 years younger than our brother, Mark. The three of us were raised by a single mother. The term people often use to describe our family dynamics is that we were raised in a broken home, but ours wasn't broken. The three of us kids were very happy, typical kids. We fought, we laughed, we cried and though out it all we had our mom. It was just the four of us.

Rob never married nor experienced the joys of fatherhood. At times I thought this was a blessing, he wasn't leaving behind small children or a wife. Then the very next thought I would feel was that he missed out on what I have always considered to be the best part of my life, my children. In retrospect I realize that had he had a family; I wouldn't have spent as much time with him in the end as I did. I treasure those moments, even though they still evoke tears and heartache.

Rob's last two years of life were the hardest for him and our family. His illness was debilitating and left him completely bedridden. So, once again, it was just the four of us; Jacquie, Mark, Rob, and Mom.

Rob's illness came on suddenly and without warning. The morning started our as normal as the morning before; mom and Rob were having coffee during breakfast before going to work. As they sat there talking, Rob lost his grip on his coffee cup. Mom thought he has spilled coffee on himself and had quickly put the cup down, but when she looked at his face, she believed he was having a stroke and called for an ambulance.

Many tests later the doctors determined that he did not have a stroke, he had a brain tumor. His tumor was located in a part of the brain that was not easily accessible, therefore it would be extremely dangerous to operate. They would need to perform a biopsy to determine whether it was cancerous. After that they could better decide what would be the best course of action.

Rob lived in Atlanta, our brother Mark lived in North Carolina, while I lived in Flint, Michigan. Once the biopsy was scheduled, I decided to drive down to offer support to our mother. It was just a biopsy, but regardless of his age, he was still our mother's baby. I did not feel that Rob was in great danger, I was going there for moral support and then I would drive home in time for work Monday. While on the operating table, Rob had a seizure. The procedure took longer than planned.

Later that evening, sitting with him and mom in his hospital room, he continued to have seizures. I timed them at one every 15 minutes. Even though his seizures only lasted a few moments, it felt like an eternity to those of us standing by, helpless, unable to help. After each seizure, Rob would lie there in his hospital bed drenched in sweat, too exhausted to even talk.

When the doctor came in to check on Rob, I told him, as I had the nurses who came every half hour to check his vitals, that he was seizing. The doctor just shrugged his shoulders. We were told that there wasn't any reason for him to be having seizures. Perhaps the trauma of surgery caused them, and they would stop once he had recovered. We weren't being given any hope at all.

The second day Rob felt well enough for short visits. My husband Jerry came in for a visit. Jerry has known Rob since he was a 13-year-old kid who bugged him to go for rides on his motorcycle and tag along on our dates. I warned my husband of the condition in which he would find Rob and to make sure that he treated him no differently than he normally would. Rob would not want us to feel sorry for him or show pity.

When he walked in, Rob was seated in a hospital chair which resembled a recliner in which he had been belted in so that he would not fall out in the event of another seizure. Right on schedule, Rob had another seizure. Trying to fill the awkward silence while we waited for the seizure to pass my mom explained to my husband that,

"Robbie is strapped in so that he won't jerk off." At the moment, in the midst of his seizure Rob's dimples appeared. I realized then that some people can hear while experiencing a seizure. He had heard mom and wanted to laugh, but his body wouldn't let him. Jerry had to look away so that he wouldn't laugh as well. Mortified I hissed,

"Mom! Jerk off is slang for masturbation!" Mom's eyes widened as her face turned red, "That's not what I meant! I meant he would fall out of his chair if he weren't strapped down!"

When his seizure was over, sweaty and trying to catch his breath, my brother gasped, "I'm lying here trying to work through this and my mom is telling people I masturbate."

Rob had to give up driving and working. The seizures continued and nothing seemed to help. Eventually, he became so weak that he was bedridden, his legs would no longer support him.

Throughout these next two years the doctors continued to shrug their shoulders and Rob continued to have seizures. My brother Mark and I wanted Rob to be treated at Duke in North Carolina, or the University of Michigan Hospital, anywhere else. Somewhere that shoulder shrugging wasn't considered an appropriate answer. Sadly, Rob was too weak to travel and wasn't being given much hope of regaining his strength. Each time I left him to travel the 753 miles home I felt guilty. I wanted to stay to help support my brother, but I had to return to my family and work.

Mark and I continued to travel to Atlanta every few weeks, staying for 3 to 4 days and returning home to attend to our family and work responsibilities. Rob became so weak that talking to us on the phone was exhausting. He could barely speak loud enough to be heard and could only hold the phone for a few moments. Phone calls caused him more frustration than they were worth. We tried FaceTime with a man both my brothers spent most of their teenage years with, Mike Creech. Sitting there with both my brothers, watching as they spoke to Mike, I realized that this was worse than talking on the phone. Still having difficulty hearing Rob speak,

Mike watched as the guy he knew as a high school swimmer struggled to form a sentence. This was Rob's first and last experience with FaceTime.

Mark and I both spent the entire last 10 days of October with Rob. Every time Mark and I went to Georgia, the three of us understood that it could be our last visit together. We tried to keep his mind occupied, but the entire time I kept worrying that we were talking about things he'd never do again or reminding him of things he used to be able to do. He never seemed upset; was never negative about things he couldn't do nor the things he wished he had done. We just talked. He enjoyed hearing us and would smile as he lay there with his eyes closed, occasionally snorting at a comment or a joke Mark made. He liked it when I read to him, and later in the evening the three of us would watch television, just like when we were kids.

There was a new series on television which I felt Rob would enjoy, "The Last Ship". Rob had been in the Navy and loved talking about his military career. I bought the first season on DVD and the three of us started watching. Rob immediately perked up and began explaining aspects of the ship to us. He explained how this ship was different than the one on which he was stationed. We even got a mini lesson on Navy rank. He only had the strength to watch half of the first episode before he fell asleep. As we left his room, Mark looked at me and said, "I am going to have to re-watch that again. Rob talked so much, I have no idea what was going on in the show." It had been a good night for Rob and for us.

A couple of days later his visiting nurse told us that she could see an improvement in him. She said that our being there was just the miracle cure he needed. My heart fell to my stomach, Mark and I were leaving the next day. We wouldn't be back until Thanksgiving. As I explained this to her the smile on her face faded, "He won't last that long."

Rob died November 11th, Veteran's Day, ten days before he would have turned 49 years old.

Although my brother did not have the opportunity to receive a healing prayer, he died knowing and having a personal loving relationship with his creator. He had joy in loving God and did not question where or why he was going.

This is why I want to tell Steve's story. I want to offer hope to others that can only be found through God's love and share the miracle I witnessed through Steve's healing.

The last thing my little brother said to me before I left his bedside for the last time was, "Do you know what I'm going to do when I die? I'm going to run through those Pearly Gates, slap St. Peter a high five, and dance."

My brother loved to dance.

Works Cited

Books
"Atwood Stadium: 75 years - 1929 -2004"
  Published by City of Flint Atwood Stadium Authority.
  June 2004

On-line Articles
American Cancer Society
https://www.cancer.org/
Flint City Baseball League is More Than Just About Baseball
 mlive.com/sports/flint/2011/07/flint_city_baseball_league_is.html
General Motors Fast Fact
  https://www.cnn.com/2014/04/08/us/general-motors-fast-facts/index.html
Guillain-Barr Syndrome
 https://www.mayoclinic.org/diseases-conditions/guillain-barre-syndrome/symptoms-causes/syc-20362793
Lary Sorensen
  https://larysorensen.info/
Remembering When GM Employed half of Flint, Michigan.
  https://tucson.com/lifestyles/remembering-when-gm-employed-half-of-flint-michigan/article_e4176079-2b6b-591e-bd13-3ca041c9dcf2.html
The Truth About Red Dye No.2
  https://www.livescience.com/35905-red-dye-no-2-truth.html
Wolff-Parkinson White Syndrome
  https://www.mayoclinic.org/diseases-conditions/wolff-parkinson-white-syndrome/symptoms-causes/syc-20354626

Made in the USA
Lexington, KY
16 November 2019